Modern Critical Interpretations

Henry James's
The Ambassadors

Modern Critical Interpretations

These and other titles in preparation

Modern Critical Interpretations

Henry James's
The Ambassadors

Edited and with an introduction by

Harold Bloom
Sterling Professor of the Humanities
Yale University

Chelsea House Publishers ◊ *1988*

NEW YORK ◊ NEW HAVEN ◊ PHILADELPHIA

© 1988 by Chelsea House Publishers, a division
of Chelsea House Educational Communications, Inc.,

Introduction © 1988 by Harold Bloom

Printed and bound in the United States of America

10 9 8 7 6 5 4 3 2 1

∞ The paper used in this publication meets the minimum
requirements of the American National Standard for
Permanence of Paper for Printed Library Materials,
Z39.48–1984.

Library of Congress Cataloging-in-Publication Data
Henry James's The ambassadors.
   (Modern critical interpretations)
   Bibliography: p.
   Includes index.
   1. James, Henry, 1843–1916. Ambassadors.
I. Bloom, Harold.   II. Series.
PS2116.A53H46   1988   813'.4   87–25623
ISBN 1-55546-006-2 (alk. paper)

Contents

Editor's Note

This book gathers together a representative selection of the best modern critical interpretations of Henry James's novel *The Ambassadors*. The critical essays are reprinted here in the chronological order of their original publication. I am grateful to Dennis Fawcett for his aid in editing this volume.

My introduction centers upon the Paterian element in Strether and suggests also some of the limitations, deliberate and indeliberate, of *The Ambassadors*. Sallie Sears begins the chronological sequence of criticism with a study of "negative imagination" in James's novel, emphasizing that "James's victims share the burden of responsibility with their victimizers" in "a kind of cooperative venture in pain."

Strether's distance from actual human relationships, accepted by him "with wit and poise," is seen by Philip M. Weinstein as the origin of Strether's curious charm. Temporality in *The Ambassadors* is analyzed by Albert A. Dunn as a vision of final loss, related to the uncertainty of the future.

Ronald Wallace argues that *The Ambassadors* is James's masterpiece, both as to form and in the depth of Strether's vision. The moral vision of Strether is articulated by Martin Price with eloquent clarity: "The sternness comes of an acceptance of consciousness, with all its privileges and pains, at the expense of all else."

The American Scene, James's own meditation upon his momentary return to his native land, is usefully juxtaposed to *The Ambassadors* by Michael Seidel. In this volume's final essay, Julie Rivkin employs Jacques Derrida's deconstructive metaphor of "the supplement" to illuminate Strether's "logic" of apparent renunciation.

Introduction

The intense critical admirers of Henry James go so far as to call him the major American writer, or even the most accomplished novelist in the English language. The first assertion neglects only Walt Whitman, while the second partly evades the marvelous sequence that moves from Samuel Richardson's *Clarissa* through Jane Austen on to George Eliot, and the alternative tradition that goes from Fielding through Dickens to Joyce. James is certainly the crucial American novelist, and in his best works the true peer of Austen and George Eliot. His precursor, Hawthorne, is more than fulfilled in the splendors of *The Portrait of a Lady* and *The Wings of the Dove,* giant descendants of *The Marble Faun,* while the rival American novelists— Melville, Mark Twain, Dreiser, Faulkner—survive comparison with James only by being so totally unlike him. Unlikeness makes Faulkner—particularly in his great phase—a true if momentary rival, and perhaps if you are to find a non-Jamesian sense of sustained power in the American novel, you need to seek out our curious antithetical tradition that moves between *Moby-Dick* and its darker descendants: *As I Lay Dying, Miss Lonelyhearts, The Crying of Lot 49.* The normative consciousness of our prose fiction, first prophesied by *The Scarlet Letter,* was forged by Henry James, whose spirit lingers not only in palpable disciples like Edith Wharton in *The Age of Innocence* and Willa Cather in her superb *A Lost Lady,* but more subtly (because merged with Joseph Conrad's aura) in novelists as various as Fitzgerald, Hemingway, and Warren. It seems clear that the relation of James to American prose fiction is precisely analogous to Whitman's relation to our poetry; each is, in his own sphere, what

1

Emerson prophesied as the Central Man who would come and change all things forever, in a celebration of the American Newness.

The irony of James's central position among our novelists is palpable, since, like the much smaller figure of T. S. Eliot later on, James abandoned his nation and eventually became a British subject, after having been born a citizen in Emerson's America. But it is a useful commonplace of criticism that James remained the most American of novelists, not less peculiarly nationalistic in *The Ambassadors* than he had been in "Daisy Miller" and *The American*. James, a subtle if at times perverse literary critic, understood very well what we continue to learn and relearn; an American writer can be Emersonian or anti-Emersonian, but even a negative stance towards Emerson always leads back again to his formulation of the post–Christian American religion of *Self*-Reliance. Overt Emersonians like Thoreau, Whitman, and Frost are no more pervaded by the Sage of Concord than are anti-Emersonians like Hawthorne, Melville, and Eliot. Perhaps the most haunted are those writers who evade Emerson, yet never leave his dialectical ambiance, a group that includes Emily Dickinson, Henry James, and Wallace Stevens.

Emerson was for Henry James something of a family tradition, though that in itself hardly accounts for the plain failure of very nearly everything that the novelist wrote about the essayist. James invariably resorts to a tone of ironic indulgence on the subject of Emerson, which is hardly appropriate to the American prophet of Power, Fate, Illusion, and Wealth. I suggest that James unknowingly mixed Emerson up with the sage's good friend Henry James, Sr., whom we dismiss as a Swedenborgian, but who might better be characterized as an American Gnostic speculator, in Emerson's mode, though closer in eminence to, say, Bronson Alcott than to the author of *The Conduct of Life*.

The sane and sacred Emerson was a master of evasions, particularly when disciples became too pressing, whether upon personal or spiritual matters. The senior Henry James is remembered now for having fathered Henry, William, and Alice, and also for his famous outburst against Emerson, whom he admired on the other side of idolatry: "O you man without a handle!"

The junior Henry James, overtly celebrating Emerson, nevertheless remarked: "It is hardly too much, or too little, to say of Emerson's writings in general that they were not composed at all."

"Composed" is the crucial word there, and makes me remember a beautiful moment in Stevens's "The Poems of Our Climate":

> There would still remain the never-resting mind,
> So that one would want to escape, come back
> To what had been so long composed.

Emerson's mind, never merely restless, indeed was never-resting, as was the mind of every member of the James family. The writings of Emerson, not composed at all, constantly come back to what had been so long composed, to what his admirer Nietzsche called the primordial poem of mankind, the fiction that we have knocked together and called our cosmos. James was far too subtle not to have known this. He chose not to know it, because he needed a provincial Emerson even as he needed a provincial Hawthorne, just as he needed a New England that never was: simple, gentle, and isolated, even a little childlike.

The days when T. S. Eliot could wonder why Henry James had not carved up R. W. Emerson seem safely past, but we ought to remember Eliot's odd complaint about James as critic: "Even in handling men whom he could, one supposes, have carved joint from joint—Emerson or Norton—his touch is uncertain; there is a desire to be generous, a political motive, an admission (in dealing with American writers) that under the circumstances this was the best possible, or that it has fine qualities." Aside from appearing to rank Emerson with Charles Eliot Norton (which is comparable to ranking Freud with Bernard Berenson), this unamiable judgment reduces Emerson, who was and is merely the mind of America, to the stature of a figure who might, at most, warrant the condescension of James (and of Eliot). The cultural polemic involved in Eliot is obvious—indeed, obsessive—and, though pleasanter in James, is really not acceptable.

> Of the three periods into which his life divides itself, the first was (as in the case of most men) that of movement, experiment and selection—that of effort too and painful probation. Emerson had his message, but he was a good while looking for his form—the form which, as he himself would have said, he never completely found and of which it was rather characteristic of him that his later years (with their growing refusal to give him the *word*), wishing to

attack him in his most vulnerable point, where his tenure was least complete, had in some degree the effect of despoiling him. It all sounds rather bare and stern, Mr. Cabot's account of his youth and early manhood, and we get an impression of a terrible paucity of alternatives. If he would be neither a farmer nor a trader he could "teach school"; that was the main resource and a part of the general educative process of the young New Englander who proposed to devote himself to the things of the mind. There was an advantage in the nudity, however, which was that, in Emerson's case at least, the things of the mind did get themselves admirably well considered. If it be his great distinction and his special sign that he had a more vivid conception of the moral life than any one else, it is probably not fanciful to say that he owed it in part to the limited way in which he saw our capacity for living illustrated. The plain, God-fearing, practical society which surrounded him was not fertile in variations: it had great intelligence and energy, but it moved altogether in the straightforward direction. On three occasions later—three journeys to Europe—he was introduced to a more complicated world; but his spirit, his moral taste, as it were, abode always within the undecorated walls of his youth. There he could dwell with that ripe unconsciousness of evil which is one of the most beautiful signs by which we know him. His early writings are full of quaint animadversion upon the vices of the place and time, but there is something charmingly vague, light and general in the arraignment. Almost the worst he can say is that these vices are negative and that his fellow-townsmen are not heroic. We feel that his first impressions were gathered in a community from which misery and extravagance, and either extreme, of any sort, were equally absent. What the life of New England fifty years ago offered to the observer was the common lot, in a kind of achromatic picture, without particular intensifications. It was from this table of the usual, the merely typical joys and sorrows that he proceeded to generalise—a fact that accounts in some degree for a certain inadequacy and thinness in his enumerations. But it helps to account also for his direct, intimate vision of the soul itself—not in its emotions, its contortions and perversions, but in its passive, exposed, yet healthy form. He knows the nature of man and the long tradition of its dangers; but we feel that whereas he can put his finger on the remedies, lying for the most part, as they do, in the deep recesses of virtue, of the spirit, he has only a kind of hearsay, uninformed acquaintance with the disorders. It would require some ingenuity, the reader may say too much, to trace closely this correspondence between his genius and the frugal, dutiful, happy but decidedly lean Boston of the past, where there was a great deal of will but very little fulcrum—like a ministry without an opposition.

The genius itself it seems to me impossible to contest— I mean the genius for seeing character as a real and supreme thing. Other writers have arrived at a more complete expression: Wordsworth and Goethe, for instance, give one a sense of having found their form, whereas with Emerson we never lose the sense that he is still seeking it. But no one has had so steady and constant, and above all so natural, a vision of what we require and what we are capable of in the way of aspiration and independence. With Emerson it is ever the special capacity for moral experience—always that and only that. We have the impression, somehow, that life had never bribed him to look at anything but the soul; and indeed in the world in which he grew up and lived the bribes and lures, the beguilements and prizes, were few. He was in an admirable position for showing, what he constantly endeavoured to show, that the prize was within. Any one who in New England at that time could do that was sure of success, of listeners and sympathy: most of all, of course, when it was a question of doing it with such a divine persuasiveness. Moreover, the way in which Emerson did it added to the charm—by word of mouth, face to face, with a rare, irresistible voice and a beautiful mild, modest authority. If Mr. Arnold is struck with the limited degree in which he was a man of letters I suppose it is because he is more struck with his having been, as it were, a man of lectures. But the lecture surely was never more purged of its grossness—the quality in it that suggests a strong light and a big brush—than as it issued from Emerson's lips; so far from being a vulgar-isation, it was simply the esoteric made audible, and instead of treating the few as the many, after the usual fashion of gentlemen on platforms, he treated the many as the few. There was probably no other society at that time in which he would have got so many persons to understand that; for we think the better of his audience as we read him, and wonder where else people would have had so much moral attention to give. It is to be remembered however that during the winter of 1847–48, on the occasion of his second visit to England, he found many listeners in London and in provincial cities. Mr. Cabot's volumes are full of evidence of the satisfactions he offered, the delights and revelations he may be said to have promised, to a race which had to seek its entertainment, its rewards, and consolations, almost exclusively in the moral world. But his own writings are fuller still; we find an instance almost wherever we open them.

It is astonishing to me that James judged Emerson's "great distinction" and "special sign" to be "that he had a more vivid conception of the moral life than any one else," unless "the moral life" has an altogether Jamesian meaning. I would rather say that the great distinction and special sign of James's fiction is that it represents a more vivid conception of the moral life than even Jane Austen or George Eliot could convey to us. Emerson is not much more concerned with morals than he is with manners; his subjects are power, freedom, and fate. As for "that ripe unconsciousness of evil" that James found in Emerson, I have not been able to find it myself, after reading Emerson almost daily for the last twenty years, and I am reminded of Yeats's late essay on Shelley's *Prometheus Unbound*, in which Yeats declares that his skeptical and passionate precursor, great poet that he certainly was, necessarily lacked the Vision of Evil. The necessity in both strong misreadings, James's and Yeats's, was to clear more space for themselves.

Jealous as I am for Emerson, I can recognize that no critic has matched James in seeing and saying what Emerson's strongest virtue is: "But no one has had so steady and constant, and above all so natural, a vision of what we require and what we are capable of in the way of aspiration and independence." No one, that is, except Henry James, for that surely is the quest of Isabel Archer towards her own quite Emersonian vision of aspiration and independence. "The moral world" is James's phrase and James's emphasis. Emerson's own emphasis, I suspect, was considerably more pragmatic than that of James. When James returned to America in 1904 on a visit, after twenty years of self-exile, he went back to Concord and recorded his impressions in *The American Scene:*

> It is odd, and it is also exquisite, that these witnessing ways should be the last ground on which we feel moved to ponderation of the "Concord school"—to use, I admit, a futile expression; or rather, I should doubtless say, it *would* be odd if there were not inevitably something absolute in the fact of Emerson's all but lifelong connection with them. We may smile a little as we "drag in" Weimar, but I confess myself, for my part, much more satisfied than not by our happy equivalent, "in American money," for Goethe and Schiller. The money is a potful in the second case as in the first, and if Goethe, in the one, represents the gold and Schiller the silver, I find (and quite putting aside any bimetallic prejudice) the same good relation in the other between Emerson and Thoreau. I open Emerson for the same benefit for which I open Goethe, the sense of moving in large intellectual space, and that of the gush, here and there, out of the rock, of the crystalline cupful, in wisdom and poetry, in Wahrheit and Dichtung; and whatever I open Thoreau for (I needn't take space here for the good reasons) I open him oftener than I open Schiller. Which comes back to our feeling that the rarity of Emerson's genius, which has made him so, for the attentive peoples, the first, and the one really rare, American spirit in letters, couldn't have spent his career in a charming woody, watery place, for so long socially and typically and, above all, interestingly homogeneous, without an effect as of the communication to it of something ineffaceable. It was during his long span his immediate concrete, sufficient world; it gave him his nearest vision of life, and he drew half his images, we recognize, from the revolution of its seasons and the play of its manners. I don't speak of

the other half, which he drew from elsewhere. It is admirably, to-day, as if we were still seeing these things *in* those images, which stir the air like birds, dim in the eventide, coming home to nest. If one had reached a "time of life" one had thereby at least heard him lecture; and not a russet leaf fell for me, while I was there, but fell with an Emersonian drop.

That is a beautiful study of the nostalgias and tells us, *contra* T. S. Eliot, what James's relation to Emerson actually was. We know how much that is essential in William James was quarried out of Emerson, particularly from the essay "Experience," which gave birth to Pragmatism. Henry James was not less indebted to Emerson than William James was. *The Portrait of a Lady* is hardly an Emersonian novel; perhaps *The Scarlet Letter* is closer to that. Yet Isabel Archer is Emerson's daughter, just as Lambert Strether is Emerson's heir. The Emersonian aura also lingers on even in the ghostly tales of Henry James.

II

James thought *The Ambassadors* was the best of all his novels. I myself prefer not only *The Portrait of A Lady* and *The Wings of the Dove,* but even *The Bostonians,* upon the simple test of rereading. All of the novelistic virtues that critics have found in *The Ambassadors* are certainly there, but they are rather too overtly there. The novel is a beautiful pattern and a model of artistic control, but is Strether of the company of Isabel Archer and Milly Theale? He is intended to be, in the best sense, James's *Portrait of a Gentleman.* Every good reader admires him and finds him sympathetic, yet across the years he comes to seem less and less memorable. I suspect that is because he does not give us enough grief; his story is not painful to us, whereas Isabel's is. Isabel, Emersonian and Paterian, nevertheless has in her the force of the Protestant will in its earlier intensity, almost the force of Dorothea Brooke, though not of their common ancestress, Clarissa Harlowe. But Lewis Lambert Strether is denied any field in which the will might be exercised heroically, since James will not even let him fall in love, except perhaps with the rather too symbolic or idealized Madame de Vionnet.

Everything in the art of Henry James is sublimely deliberate, which means that the imbalance between the matter and the manner of *The Ambassadors* is James's peculiar mode of taking those ultimate risks that alone allow him to make distinctions and achieve distinction. Strether's mission is to rescue Chad from Madame de Vionnet, but is Chad worth rescuing? The best thing about Chad is that he becomes Horatio to Strether's Hamlet, and so serves as the reader's surrogate for appreciating Strether. However, Horatio floats about the court of Elsinore as a kind of privileged outsider, and his splendid destiny is to survive as the teller of Hamlet's story. Chad will go back to Woollett and enthusiastically pioneer in the art of advertising so as to raise the Newsome domestic device to undreamed-of heights of use and profit. The irony of irony is all very well in high romance or in High Romanticism, but not even the comic sense of Henry James quite saves *The Ambassadors* from a certain readerly listlessness that follows Strether's terminal "Then there we are!" to the endlessly receptive Maria Gostrey.

James is perfectly ruthless in his application of what has come to be the Formalist principle that subject matter in literary art is precisely what does not matter. The *Iliad* after all, from any ironic perspective, like that of Shakespeare's more than mordant *Troilus and Cressida,* has as its matter the quarrels between brawny and vainglorious chieftains over the possession of the whore Helen, or of this or that despoiled captive woman. That is not Homer's *Iliad,* nor is *The Ambassadors* the story of the education of Lambert Strether, until at last he can warn little Bilham (one wearies of the "little"!) that life's meaning is that we must *live. Seeing* is living, for Strether, as for James, as for Carlyle, for Ruskin, for Emerson, for Pater.

"Impressionism," as a literary term, is not very useful, since even Pater is not an Impressionist in a painterly sense. What Strether *sees* is simply what is there, and what is there would appear to be loss, very much in Pater's sense of loss. James's aesthetic has its differences from Pater's, but I am not so certain that Strether's vision and Pater's are easily to be distinguished from one another. When Strether experiences his crisis (or epiphany) in Gloriani's garden, we are in the cosmos of Pater and of Nietzsche, in which life can be justified only as an aesthetic phenomenon. Strether has just met Madame de Vionnet for the first time: "She was dressed in black, but in black that struck him as light and transparent; she was exceedingly fair, and, though she was as markedly slim, her face had a roundness, with eyes far apart and a little strange." Perhaps that is love at first sight, and certainly Madame de Vionnet is herself the epiphany. "In black that struck him as light and transparent" would have alerted any Emersonian or Paterian, and this is the prelude to the central paragraph of *The Ambassadors,* Strether's famous address to little Bilham:

> "It's not too late for *you,* on any side, and you don't strike me as in danger of missing the train; besides which people can be in general pretty well trusted, of course—with the clock of their freedom ticking as loud as it seems to do here—to keep an eye on the fleeting hour. All the same don't forget that you're young—blessedly young; be glad of it on the contrary and live up to it. Live all you can; it's a mistake not to. It doesn't so much matter what you do in particular, so long as you have your life. If you haven't had that what *have* you had? This place and these impressions— mild as you may find them to wind a man up so; all my impressions of Chad and of people I've seen at *his* place— well, have had their abundant message for me, have just dropped *that* into my mind. I see it now. I haven't done so enough before—and now I'm old; too old at any rate for what I see. Oh I *do* see, at least; and more than you'd believe or I can express. It's too late. And it's as if the train had fairly waited at the station for me without my having had the gumption to know it was there. Now I hear its faint receding whistle miles and miles down the line. What one loses one loses; make no mistake about that. The affair—I mean the affair of life—couldn't, no doubt, have been different for me; for it's at the best a tin mould, either fluted and embossed, with ornamental excrescences, or else smooth and dreadfully plain, into which, a helpless jelly, one's consciousness is poured—so that one 'takes' the form, as the great cook says, and is more or less compactly held by it: one lives in fine as one can. Still, one has the illusion of freedom; therefore don't be, like me, without the memory of that illusion. I was either, at the right time, too stupid or too intelligent to have it; I don't quite know which. Of course at present I'm a case of reaction against the mistake; and the voice of reaction should, no doubt,

always be taken with an allowance. But that doesn't affect the point that the right time is now yours. The right time is *any* time that one is still so lucky as to have. You've plenty; that's the great thing; you're, as I say, damn you, so happily and hatefully young. Don't at any rate miss things out of stupidity. Of course I don't take you for a fool, or I shouldn't be addressing you thus awfully. Do what you like so long as you don't make *my* mistake. For it was a mistake. Live!" . . . Slowly and sociably, with full pauses and straight dashes, Strether had so delivered himself; holding little Bilham from step to step deeply and gravely attentive. The end of all was that the young man had turned quite solemn, and that this was a contradiction of the innocent gaiety the speaker had wished to promote. He watched for a moment the consequence of his words, and then, laying a hand on his listener's knee and as if to end with the proper joke: "And now for the eye I shall keep on you!"

The loud ticking of the clock of freedom is Strether's version of Pater's "We have an interval, and then our place knows us no more," itself a Paterian commentary upon Victor Hugo's "We are all condemned men, with a kind of indefinite reprieve." Pater's question is how are we to spend that interval, and his answer is in perception and sensation as memorialized by art. Strether is not a questioner because Pater is a theoretician of seeing, but Strether *does* see, indeed always has seen, but was too morally intelligent to have had the illusion of freedom at the right time. And yet: "The right time is *any* time that one is still so lucky as to have." James calls Strether elderly, at fifty-five, but even in 1903 that was not necessarily elderly. Strether, like Pater's Mona Lisa, is older than the rocks among which he sits, or he is like Nietzsche's Emerson: "He does not know how old he is already, or how young he is still going to be." James's way of expressing that Nietzschean paradox has less wit but more American pragmatism. Strether, like Emerson, is a man of imagination who achieves "an amount of experience out of any proportion to his adventures." There truly is no past for Strether; he is an intuitive Emersonian who knows that there is no history, only biography. Strether has seen in Madame de Vionnet what Pater saw in Leonardo's Lady Lisa (I owe this insight to F. O. Matthiessen): a goddess, a nymph, a woman-of-women, infinitely nuanced, end-lessly varied.

But if Strether has fallen in love with his vision, his love is like the love of Pater or of Henry James himself, a wholly aesthetic phenomenon. We do not expect to see Strether replace Chad as the lady's lover any more than we could expect him to settle down with the accommodating Maria Gostrey, let alone attempt to marry Mrs. Newsome upon his return to Woollett. The sad truth is that none of these ladies, not even the superbly unreal Madame de Vionnet, would be adequate to Lewis Lambert Strether, anymore than Touchett, Warburton, Goodwood would be adequate to Isabel Archer. Strether at least does not suffer a female version of Osmond, but then Strether is hardly the heir of all the ages. He is the surrogate for Henry James, novelist, who inevitably preferred his own spiritual self-portrait to all his other novels.

The Negative Imagination: *The Ambassadors*

Sallie Sears

Like Paris, the great "jewel" that is its setting, *The Ambassadors* has a rare iridescence, luminosity of surface, and wealth of association. Though milder and more muted than *The Wings of the Dove* or *The Golden Bowl,* it is the most elaborate and richly textured of James's dramas of moral consciousness. It is unique too among the late works in its focus upon middle age (the "afternoon," the "twilight of life") rather than youth, for though the theme of youth is a predominant one in the book, our center of attention is a character far past that period in his life. In these respects—and perhaps in others—*The Ambassadors* has a certain spiritual kinship with *The Tempest*. Like Prospero, Strether is exiled temporarily from his native ground into a place of enchantment:

> In the garden of the Tuileries he had lingered, on two or three spots, to look; it was as if the wonderful Paris spring had stayed him as he roamed. The prompt Paris morning struck its cheerful notes—in a soft breeze and a sprinkled smell, in the light flit, over the garden-floor, of bareheaded girls. . . . The air had a taste as of something mixed with art, something that presented nature as a white-capped master-chef.

From *The Negative Imagination: Form and Perspective in the Novels of Henry James.* © 1968 by Cornell University. Cornell University Press, 1968.

All three of the late novels make deliberate use of the fairy-tale mode: motifs of enchantment, spells, figurative or real princesses and princes, sorcerers, and fairy godmothers. But in none of the three is this mode used in so sustained and at the same time so quiet a way as in *The Ambassadors*, where it is an important yet unobtrusive element affecting the tone and texture of the entire novel. The air is "charged," "infectious": "Poor Strether had . . . to recognise the truth that wherever one paused in Paris the imagination reacted before one could stop it." And the texture woven by the imagination in this novel is elaborate, complex, and lustrous. "I dare say . . . , [remarks Maria] that I do, that we all do here, run too much to mere eye. But how can it be helped? We're all looking at each other—and in the light of Paris one sees what things resemble. That's what the light of Paris seems always to show. It's the fault of the light of Paris—dear old light!"

Part of the complexity, the richness of *The Ambassadors* is in fact directly due to the conscious utilization of the principle of "resemblance," the yoking together of heterogeneous associations and areas of experience through the unifying medium of Strether's consciousness. Everything that Strether sees is a kind of haunt, a presence that suggests or evokes the quality of another presence, usually one that is gone irretrievably, or even one that was never there but only yearned for. In England, his first taste of "Europe," he strolls and pauses "here and there for a dismantled gate or a bridged gap, with rises and drops, steps up and steps down, queer twists, queer contacts, peeps . . . under the brows of gables," and his reaction is one of intense pleasure coupled with immediate evocation of the past: "Too deep almost for words was the delight of these things to Strether; yet as deeply mixed with it were certain images of his inward picture. He had trod this walk in the far-off time, at twenty-five." And what in turn had been the feelings that accompanied him then, in his first and youthful sojourn: the need and yearning to utilize the experience as a creative foundation for his future life. This reaction "consecrated"—declared sacred—the significance of that early pilgrimage, and took the form of a "private pledge of his own to treat the occasion as a relation formed with the higher culture and see that, as they said at Woollett, it should bear a good harvest." But the pledge remained unfulfilled, so that the color of his *present* experience becomes a bleak sense of all "the promises to himself that he had after his other visit never kept," "mere sallow paint on the door of the temple of taste that he had dreamed of raising up."

This coupling of immediate, vivid sensory detail with the sense of the significance it might have had but didn't and now never can—of present unobtainable riches and past irrevocable bankruptcy—is the characteristic mode of perception in *The Ambassadors*. Strether defines it in himself as a tendency to "uncontrolled perceptions," by which he means not that his mind is a jungle watering-ground, but that his sense of personal privation is irrepressible and that he would be happier if it weren't. So he sits with Maria Gostrey in England at a small table with rose-colored shades on the lighted candles and recalls that he had been "to the theatre, even to the opera, in Boston, with Mrs. Newsome . . . but there had been no little confronted dinner, no pink lights, no whiff of vague sweetness, as a preliminary." Maria's dress, low at bosom and shoulders, and her throat circled with a broad red velvet band do not serve—directly—as an incentive to lust but rather as a "rueful" recollection that "Mrs. Newsome's dress was never in any degree 'cut down,' and she never wore round her throat a broad red velvet band." He then begins to think what that lady *did* wear (an Elizabethan ruche), conscious of his own mental processes yet helpless to control them. Every immediate impression of any intensity that Strether has, serves, like the red band, "as a starting-point for fresh backward, fresh forward, fresh lateral flights."

What Strether's consciousness both depicts and exemplifies here is the metaphoric imagination, the consistent presentation of which is largely responsible for the rich texture and thematic complexity of the novel. In addition, the statement the figures repeatedly make—"this is a symbol of all that I never had and never will"—determines the book's tone of bemused melancholy and passive yearning. We know that James wanted his protagonist to be "*fine,* clever, literary almost" and that he considered but rejected making him a novelist (both on the grounds that that would be too much like William Dean Howells, whose impassioned plea to a mutual friend to "live" provided James the theme of *The Ambassadors*, and on the grounds that such a hero generally would be too improbable). James also rejected the possibility of making him an artist, because an artist, like a journalist, lawyer, or doctor "WOULD in a manner have 'lived.'" But these considerations of a creative "type," though waived, are significant, and his hero eventually was to be, in spite of his personal shortcomings and his failure to achieve an identity through work, a man of imagination.

And the paradox of his character—the man of imagination who is at the same time a New England puritan—is a central paradox, of which the European-American antithesis is but one symbolic projection. Strether, we are warned at the outset, is burdened "with the oddity of a double consciousness. There was detachment in his zeal and curiosity in his indifference." In the immediate context, this refers to his ambivalence at the prospect of meeting Waymarsh, whose presence he wishes for yet whose absence he enjoys "extremely." But the broader context is the significance this meeting has for Strether, for Waymarsh is the true American representative, who is second only to the unseen yet ubiquitous Mrs. Newsome. He is an original specimen of the most typical New World genus: "a truly majestic aboriginal," the Great Father, the "American statesman . . . trained in 'Congressional halls,' of an elder day." The delay in their meeting means for Strether "such a consciousness of personal freedom as he hadn't known for years," freedom to give over "his afternoon and evening to the immediate and the sensible."

It is of course because Waymarsh is the externalization of one of Strether's inward voices that he dreads meeting him. If Strether did not have susceptibilities of conscience against his own delight in the "immediate and the sensible," he would feel no alarm. Not only does he have them, however, but they increase in intensity with the amount of pleasure he feels, so that strolling in the early morning of Paris, which hangs before him, "the vast bright Babylon, like some huge iridescent object, a jewel brilliant and hard . . . twinkled and trembled and melted together . . . all surface one moment . . . all depth the next," he is tormented with a kind of moral uneasiness. It takes the form of a rhetorical problem: "Was it at all possible . . . to like Paris enough without liking it too much?" The implicit accusation of course is that *any* liking is, by definition, "too much"—and Strether does like it.

This war between the sense of rectitude and the sense of beauty is the basic conflict of the novel, as it is the basic conflict of Strether's character; indeed the former is simply an extension or elaboration of the latter. The book is not about Europe and America, or even about Europeans and Americans. It is about the significance that each place and its inhabitants have for a man burdened with "a double consciousness." What we are given is a complex study not in twofold but in fourfold reactions, for Strether is ambivalent to *both* of the great civilizations that are the symbolic terrain of his own internal struggle. It is by no means just Europe to which his responses are divided, though that continent is the actual setting of the events of the novel and is indeed Babylon to his feelings: place of iniquity, home of whores, yet precious beyond words, a temple, like Maria Gostrey's nest, to "the lust of the eyes and the pride of life."

Though James typically is concerned with the *relation* of consciousness to the external human scene, finding in aspects of the latter analogues for the former (or items of special significance to it), the nature of that scene becomes progressively more abstract in each of the last three novels until, in *The Golden Bowl,* the external world has receded as an "interesting" tactile and visual field (with a few exceptions such as the scene of the purchase of the bowl in the shop). The source of particularity, the texture of sensuous surfaces in that novel, comes instead primarily from the luminous, elaborate metaphors by means of which the characters through whose eyes the story is seen objectify their perceptions. That work also achieves particularity by means of tableaux in which the choreography of the principal characters—physical movements of slow pursuit along a terrace, "significant" regroupings around a table, and so forth—are at one and the same time symbolic of various games of manipulation and deceit being played among them and the literal means by which the "play" becomes actuality and the deceit (or whatever) accomplished, ratified. Such scenes are "vivid," theatrical, and in them the outer world does figure, but rather more in the manner of a stage setting, a backdrop, than as a projection of three-dimensional eternal reality in which the characters are continuously "located."

In *The Ambassadors* (completed before but published after *The Wings of the Dove*), however, the "setting"—though as we have indicated it stands in analogic relation to conflicting aspects of Strether's consciousness—*is* projected in its three-dimensionality and detailed concreteness. The drama of the hero's sensibility takes place in a context of intensely vivid social realities—attitudes, customs, modes of thought and behavior, American speech and dress, Parisian gardens, streets, interior landscapes—which have *both* an extrinsic and an intrinsic relation to that sensibility.

In the novel we are given an extended ironic characterization of middle-class American and upper-class Parisian culture, "a comic work" as it has been observed [by Richard Chase], "in the general tradition of Molière and Jane Austen." At the same time, however, its scope is far broader, its range of tone more complex than the typical "novel of manners." The effectiveness of Jane Austen's work, for example, largely depends upon the unquestioned acceptance of a fixed social and ethical code of behavior, deviations from which can be examined with minute exactness. But *The Ambassadors* has for its framework not one but two such codes, in radical opposition, neither of which in the final analysis completely triumphs or is completely defeated. It is in the study of half-victories and partial defeats of two world views as they relate to the personal history of Lambert Strether that the significance of the novel lies, for whatever its context, it is first and last his story. The lives of the other characters, as well as the cultural settings in which they take place, have meaning for us only as they have meaning for Strether, whose feelings, responses, perceptions, and reactions constitute the subject matter of the book.

So that the pertinent question is the nature of the relationship between the European-American dichotomy in the novel and the private life of Lambert Strether, the "ambassador" on a temporary mission from Woollett, Massachusetts, to Paris, France. The nature of his mission, as we know, is to fetch back to the bosom of his home, family, and "business" young Chad Newsome, whose protracted stay in Paris, it is believed in Woollett, means that he is in the clutches of an immoral woman. What actually happens in the book is in a sense relatively simple: Strether undergoes two major shifts in his attitude toward his mission. Initially he is fully primed with the Woollett concept—that the female in question, whoever she is, is not "even an apology for a decent woman"—and considers it of the greatest importance that Chad at once break with everything and return straight home. The first shift comes after he encounters both Chad, who has changed in manner and appearance from a condition of relative mediocrity to one of relative magnificence, and Madame de Vionnet, who, a little to his disappointment, has nothing about her of the tart he had expected. Impressed by Chad, charmed by Madame de Vionnet, Strether comes to the conclusion, in which he is abetted by overt statements from both Chad himself and the latter's friend little Bilham, that the attachment between the couple is a "virtuous" one and that Chad must therefore not desert her. The second shift comes when he discovers after a chance meeting with the couple in the French countryside that their attachment is *not* "virtuous," that it is sexual, and that he has been deceived. But by then, sick and disillusioned though he is—"It was the quantity of make-believe involved and so vividly exemplified that most disagreed with his spiritual stomach"—something of major significance has happened to Strether's concept of "virtue." His final stance is that even though the affair is not only sexual but adulterous, Chad would be "a criminal of the deepest dye" to abandon a woman who had aided him so, who has sacrificed so much for him, and who loves him so. "You owe her everything," he tells Chad at the end, "very much more than she can ever owe you. You've in other words duties to her, of the most positive sort; and I don't see what other duties—as the others are presented to you—can be held to go before them."

This essentially is the plot of the novel, and upon those two simple shifts in Strether's attitude hangs a tale half comic, half tragic, certainly pathetic, of the struggle of a complex and somewhat befuddled psyche to find, before it is too late, some meaning, significance, and beauty in life. One might say that the book is about how he almost finds it: almost, but not quite.

Europe and America each offers to Strether its own modus vivendi, its own elaborately articulated set of possibilities and philosophy of existence. That the basic assumptions of each are violently antithetical is something that Strether at first accepts as a matter of course, then in his hopeful delusion about "virtuous attachments" discards, then comes again painfully to recognize. But by that time a strange and complex interaction of the two styles of life has taken place within Strether, with the result that each has operated upon the other with something of the effect of a slow poison. He is left in the end with a lingering distaste—coupled with a nostalgia for the beauty that was almost truth too—for both places, a permanent spiritual exile, in possession only of the rather pathetic consolation that he had "not, out of the whole affair," got anything for himself and has therefore, in some obscure but honorable way, been "right."

The great values upheld and cherished by Woollett are conformity, which passes as "equality," and rectitude. There are but two "types" in Woollett, the male and the female, and on any subject whatsoever but "two or three" opinions. One of Strether's first impressions of Europe is his sense of the multifold discriminations, rankings, and categories that, by contrast, are indulged in there. Miss

Gostrey, he recognizes, was "the mistress of a hundred cases or categories, receptacles of the mind, subdivisions for convenience, in which, from a full experience, she pigeon-holed her fellow mortals with a hand as free as that of a compositor scattering type. She was as equipped in this particular as Strether was the reverse." This concept of "personal types" becomes the keynote of Europe for Strether, part of whose growth of experience consists in his increasing ability to recognize them when he sees them. But the significant thing is the concept itself, the very notion of a hierarchical ordering of values, rather than the degree of skill he shows in its practical application. It is a concept regarded with the profoundest mistrust and abhorrence by the sister communities and companions-at-arms, Milrose, Connecticut, and Woollett, Massachusetts, for it reeks of political and spiritual decadence, the old order, and the old, castoff world. Its great emblem is the Catholic Church: "The Catholic Church, for Waymarsh—that was to say the enemy, the monster of bulging eyes and far-reaching quivering groping tentacles—was exactly society, exactly the multiplication of shibboleths, exactly the discrimination of types and tones, exactly the wicked old Rows of Chester, rank with feudalism; exactly in short Europe."

But what does it mean for the errant Strether? The chain of his association that leads to this perception of what Europe means to Waymarsh is significant here. The two of them, with Miss Gostrey, are strolling and gazing into shop windows, Waymarsh maintaining "an ambiguous dumbness that might have represented either the growth of a perception or the despair of one" and looking "guilty and furtive" when his eye happens to be caught by some object of minor interest. Strether, however, is utterly entranced and apologizes for his rapture on the grounds of previous deprivation: "Do what he might . . . his previous virtue was still there, and it seemed fairly to stare at him out of the windows of shops that were not as the shops of Woollett, fairly to make him want things that he shouldn't know what to do with. It was by the oddest, the least admissible of laws demoralising him now; and the way it boldly took was to make him want more wants." He and Miss Gostrey find themselves disposed to talk as "society" talks, and discuss clothing, passers-by, faces, types: "Was what was happening to himself then . . . really that a woman of fashion was floating him into society and that an old friend deserted on the brink was watching the force of the current?" She allows him to buy a pair of gloves, and it is then that he realizes that for Waymarsh "mere discriminations about a pair of gloves" is emblematic of the fundamental wantonness of Europe and that Strether for indulging in such discriminations is like a "Jesuit in petticoats, a representative of the recruiting interests of the Catholic Church."

What we have here is a complex set of associations and significances, all stemming from the single concept of "type," and having implications of a very broad range indeed. One of the most pertinent of these implications is the connection between that aspect of experience involving the making of "discriminations" and the phenomenon of taste. For a hierarchical ordering of values is a necessary condition of the latter: without it a sense of what is fitting, harmonious, or beautiful is impossible. That Strether applies it at the moment to a pair of gloves instead of, say, a painting is beside the point. What matters is the phenomenon itself: it is one of the possibilities of life that Europe offers and that America denies him.

Closely connected to the notion of taste—indeed an intricate part of it—is the whole realm of fluid, sensuous experience, of "sensible impressions and agreeable sensations," of strolls "where the low-browed galleries were darkest, the opposite gables queerest, the solicitations of every kind densest." It was the delight of such that was "too deep almost for words" for Strether as he wandered earlier with Miss Gostrey, just as it is Waymarsh's present source of guilt and furtiveness when in spite of himself his eye happens to linger upon some interesting object. But if Strether's reaction had been merely delight, we would have a different novel; in fact, he shares with his fellow New Englander the pain of a stricken conscience, the inability wholly to give himself over to the flux of immediate experience. With Miss Gostrey he feels "as if this were wrong"; he labels the feeling "the terror. . . . I'm always considering something else; something else, I mean, than the thing of the moment. The obsession of the other thing is the terror." At the same time, he longs "unspeakably" to escape the obsession, goes so far as to beg her to help him do so.

Now this "failure to enjoy" is a "general" failure, as Strether tells Maria: it is not a personal flaw in either himself or Waymarsh, but rather an habitual trait of the New England conscience whose responses are dictated by the moral imperatives of "ought" and "ought not" (Woollett "isn't sure it ought to enjoy. If it were it would"). Woollett of course is in no such state of uncertainty as

Strether pretends with respect to the lust of the eyes. Woollett is perfectly sure it ought not to enjoy: after all it is the New Testament, not the Old, that requests us to pluck out our right eye if it offends us. The direct biblical connection is with the sin of adultery, as it is reinterpreted by Christ to involve desire as well as action: "But I say unto you, That whosoever looketh on a woman to lust after her hath committed adultery with her already in his heart" (Matt. 5:28). But the Sermon on the Mount mentions the eye in another connection too: with respect to its yearning for mammon and the treasures of the earth, which "moths and rust doth corrupt." The use of wealth specifically for food, drink, and clothing is condemned: "And why take ye thought for raiment? Consider the lilies of the field. . . . Even Solomon in all his glory was not arrayed like one of these." Poor Strether and his pair of gloves; no wonder he is painfully aware that Waymarsh considers him not only "sophisticated" and "worldly" but also "wicked," the three indeed being, to the New England conscience, synonymous. Later this is made explicit as it comes to Strether "somehow to and fro that what poor Waymarsh meant was 'I told you so—that you'd lose your immortal soul!' "

So one of the dilemmas Strether is in as a man of taste burdened with puritan leanings is that the very things which most gratify his sensibility are the ones which most distress his conscience. Though he does not think (except ironically) in orthodox theological terms, he has internalized the trappings of Protestantism to the extent that his consciousness of the agreeable is continually marred by his consciousness of sin. Hence, he never has an unambiguous reaction to the delights of Paris: making a "frantic friend" of little Bilham, finding himself moved and pleased by, if not envious of, the latter's tranquillity, he still thinks: "It was by little Bilham's amazing serenity that he had at first been affected, but he had inevitably, in his circumspection, felt it as the trail of the serpent, the corruption, as he might conveniently have said, of Europe." At the same time, Paris continually seduces him: it makes him "want more wants," it gives him a taste of "personal freedom" such as he has not known for years, accompanied by "the full sweetness of the taste of leisure," fills him with "that apprehension of the interesting" totally unavailable in Woollett, Massachusetts, offers to him the "delicate and appetising" effects of tone and tint. The effect of this split response is that as his exposure to Paris deepens, both sides of his conflict intensify. The purity, the rectitude, the reliability of the American character become something he yearns more and more to find in its European counterpart, while the flatness, the Philistinism, the inflexibility of the former grow increasingly distasteful to him, just as his suspicion of the Parisian serpent enlarges as its seductive powers more and more envelop him. He is becoming at one and the same time more alienated from and more involved with both civilizations.

The focus of this conflict is the relationship between Chad and Madame de Vionnet and the nature of Strether's own role with respect to it. Whatever his other inward inconsistencies, Strether is consistent in always living by his sense of duty. In the beginning, this sense is identical with Woollett's, but what happens in the book is a great swing from a public to a private conscience, from an established, predetermined, black-and-white, fixed code of conduct to a personal, flexible, more relativist code in which each case is judged by its own merits. This shift is foreshadowed early in the novel, in a conversation with Maria:

> "You've accepted the mission of separating him from the wicked woman. Are you quite sure she's very bad for him?"
>
> Something in his manner showed it as quite pulling him up. "Of course we are. Wouldn't *you* be?"
>
> "Oh, I don't know. One never does—does one?—beforehand. One can only judge on the facts. Yours are quite new to me."

Madame de Vionnet's "case" in Woollett's eyes is precisely that of a violator of a general code. Woollett's reasoning is syllogistic, deductive: all fornicators (they don't yet know that she is an adulteress) are immoral, Madame de Vionnet is a fornicator, therefore she is immoral. Strether, confronted with the example in the flesh and also by this time deeply involved in his own conflicting responses to Europe, is forced to reexamine his premises and ultimately to reason inductively. But it happens in a queer, roundabout way: in his attempt to reconcile the irreconcilable, he denies the *second* premise, not the first, until the bitter end. In so doing, he is able for a while to cling to the ethical system (absolute right and wrong, which are knowable) upon which he was reared, and thus to find the goodness that is America in the very heart of the charm that is Europe. What is at stake is considerably more than the possibility of an error of judgment about the nature of a given relationship: it is a whole way of life, an entire system of thought, belief, and behavior, a set of assumptions about the nature and significance of existence. He abandons the assumption of absolute right and wrong only when he is forced to, and comes finally to equate "virtue" with concepts other than celibacy; but it is a private equation he arrives at, a lonely one, one that Woollett would never accept in a thousand years. Madame de Vionnet always remains charming to him, but her virtue does not consist in her charm (at least not to his moral, though admittedly to his aesthetic, sense). It consists rather in her personal sacrifice to Chad: the devotion and love she has poured on him, the assistance she has rendered him, the man she has more or less made out of unpromising raw materials. It is not that Woollett would not recognize these as desirable attributes in a wife; but in a mistress they are merely further symptoms of wantonness.

Strether's personal moral history with respect to his attitude toward Madame de Vionnet is a reenactment of a change in American cultural patterns that took place in the nineteenth century; the breakdown of the old puritanical code of conscience and the establishment of a new, freer, more relativistic code. The change in each case was for much the same reason: the old canon did not fit all situations, was too harsh, tended to ignore human considerations and distort the truth. So James writes [in the preface to *The Ambassadors*], "*The* false position, for our belated man of the world . . . was obviously to have presented himself at the gate of that boundless menagerie primed with a moral scheme of the most approved pattern which was yet framed to break down on any approach to vivid facts; that is to any at all liberal appreciation of them."

What then is the difference between Strether and Chad, whose moral transportations may be said to be similar, at least up to a point? The difference is significant in its intuition of two divergent trends in American culture, both of which are connected with the breakdown of the puritan standard of ethics. Chad's relativism leads him directly into opportunism, manipulation, and exploitation: it is he who is the advertising man of the future. Strether's relativism on the other hand leads him to a struggle for a code of honor outside any system, to some private ideal of selflessness and personal allegiance, the significance of human ties, of intimacy, passion, and pain. The New England conscience had its strengths as well as its weaknesses, and one of its strengths was the sanctioning of the idea of behavior based upon responsibility toward one's fellows. This Strether preserves all the way through, though its form, significance, and finality have altered for him by the time the events have run their course.

But there are other differences between Strether and Chad too, not the least of which is that Chad is "the young man marked out by women." Once again, Strether's associations in connection with this perception are pertinent, as they link different areas of experience that together form part of the significance of his European adventure. Chad, he recognizes in their first conversation, not only is handsomer than he remembers him, but also is completely made over. His manners are "formed," he is a gentleman and man of the world, in other words "a man to whom things had happened and were variously known." Like a work of art, he has "a form and a surface," a design, tone, accent. His "identity so rounded off" and his "massive young manhood" hint at "some self-respect." It occurs then to Strether that the proper designation for this young man marked out by women is that of an "irreducible young Pagan." The qualities of Chad's Parisian sea change thus are sophistication, worldliness, taste, youth, and potency: a sensuous, polished surface and a sexual, pagan nature.

And in spite of Strether's sense of duty, his insistence that the only way he can be "right" is to get nothing out of the whole affair for himself, he does have a personal investment in the lives of Chad Newsome and Madame de Vionnet. They represent for him his last chance to "live," through vicarious participation in their experiences. His capitulation to and defense of them (and therefore, by extension, of Europe) is, he confesses to Maria, his "surrender," his "tribute" to youth: "It has to come in somewhere, if only out of the lives, the conditions, the feelings of other persons. . . . The point is that they're mine. Yes, they're my youth; since somehow at the right time nothing else ever was."

Strether thus joins the long list of characters in James, those who achieve their strongest emotional satisfactions by observing and sometimes manipulating the lives of others: the Olive Chancellors, Susan Stringhams, Fanny Assinghams, and Ralph Touchetts. The type reaches its apotheosis in *The Portrait of a Lady,* in the figure of Gilbert Osmond, who literally cannot survive without a host, in vacuum, and whose whole identity is determined by the opinion of that shifting and nebulous personality known as "society." ("I *am* convention," he tells Isabel at one point.) And certainly Strether partakes of the characteristics of this type, though he is a very different breed of it from Osmond. Like Osmond, however, he has no coherent inward sense of himself ("He was Lambert Strether because he was on the cover, whereas it should have been, for anything like glory, that he was on the cover because he was Lambert Strether"); like Ralph, in his twilight hours he makes a bid for a degree of personal pleasure by vicariously investing his feeling. Strether's rationale for the attempt is not unlike Ralph's either: it is "too late" for him to act on his own behalf: the most he can do is to act on and through others, in an oblique attempt to find the youth he himself never had.

The Ambassadors has been objected to precisely on the grounds of Strether's passivity and the vicarious quality of his experience, with critics remarking that these attributes are responsible for a certain attenuated quality about the novel that persists in spite of its obvious charm. Richard Chase writes [in *Twelve Original Essays*] that the "general lack of masculine reciprocation, especially in Strether himself, accounts in part for the somewhat tenuous quality—the softness at the center—of life as depicted in James' novel . . . despite the wealth of reported observation," and then goes on to compare (a comparison he acknowledges is invidious) the novel unfavorably with *Antony and Cleopatra*. And [F. O.] Matthiessen writes,

> The burden of *The Ambassadors* is that Strether has awak-
> ened to a wholly new sense of life. Yet he does nothing at
> all to fulfill that sense. Therefore, fond as James is of him,
> we cannot help feeling his relative emptiness. At times,
> even . . . it is forced upon us that, despite James' humorous
> awareness of the inadequacy of his hero's adventures,
> neither Strether nor his creator escape a certain soft
> fussiness.
>
> (*Henry James: The Major Phase*)

Such remarks come down to a moral—not aesthetic—demand that a novelist conceive of his characters in terms of the most dubious banalities: unexamined cultural stereotypes having to do with "masculinity," aggressiveness, and so forth. Behind this in turn lies a conception of art based on standards lifted without examination from realistic fiction: art should directly engage and passionately move the spectator by its imitation of the texture of daily life, its representation of "real" (in this case sexually vigorous) three-dimensional people.

James himself of course repeatedly insists upon the intimate connection between art and life. In the preface to *The Portrait of a Lady,* he emphasizes "the perfect dependence of the 'moral' sense of a work of art on the amount of felt life concerned in producing it" and in the preface to *The Ambassadors,* he writes, "Art deals with what we see, it must first contribute full-handed that ingredient; it plucks its material . . . in the garden of life—which material else-where grown is stale and uneatable." But the amount of "felt life" evoked comes down ultimately to "the artist's prime sensibility," the "quality and capacity" of which represent the work's "projected morality." This attribute itself is finally viewed by James as "some mark made on the intelligence." In other words, the measure of "life" in a work of art for James turns out to be the intensity and complexity of the consciousness that is operating upon the material it receives from the external world. From this vantage point, notions like "masculine reciprocity" are not only irrelevant but needlessly confusing: they tell us nothing about James's art for better or for worse, and ask us to bring to bear upon that art standards that obscure, not clarify, its nature.

In the case of Strether, James determined to make his a drama of consciousness rather than of action in part because of

> the dreadful little old tradition, one of the platitudes of the human comedy, that people's moral scheme *does* break down in Paris. . . . [and to avoid the platitude James decided] The revolution performed by Strether under the influence of the most interesting of great cities was to have nothing to do with any *bêtise* of the imputably "tempted" state; he was to be thrown forward, rather, thrown quite with violence, upon his lifelong trick of intense reflexion.
>
> (R. P. Blackmur, ed., *The Art of the Novel: Critical Prefaces*)

Moreover, while it is true enough in a sense that "the burden" of the novel is that its hero "has awakened to a wholly new sense of life," the fact that he does not fulfill himself is not a lapse on James's part but is, on the contrary, deliberate. Speaking of Strether's cry to little Bilham to "live"—which is both the "germ" of the novel and an "independent particle" lurking "in [its] mass"—James writes, he has accordingly missed too much, though perhaps after all constitutionally qualified for a much better part, and he wakes up to it in conditions that press the spring of a terrible question. *Would* there yet perhaps be time for reparation?—reparation, that is, for the injury done his character; for the affront, he is quite ready to say, so stupidly put upon it and in which he has even himself had so clumsy a hand? The answer to which is that he now at all events *sees;* so that the business of my tale and the march of my action, not to say the precious moral of everything, is just my demonstration of this process of vision.

(*The Art of the Novel*)

James answers obliquely the question whether Strether would have enough time to make up for all he has missed, and the answer is negative: there isn't enough time, but at least Strether sees—what he has missed and that it is too late for reparation. Like his creator, he "was to go without many things, ever so many—as all persons do in whom contemplation takes so much the place of action." The excruciation of the novel, its intensity, is precisely *due to* the contrast between Strether's awakened sense of what might have been and what is—or, to put it another way, his awareness that what might have been and what can never be are one and the same. The blow to him is total: the past is undone, the future without promise, the present both a reminder and a measure of both.

Matthiessen comes much closer to an objective and sensitive view of James's art and its relation to life earlier in his study when he writes, apropos of James's fascination with "seeing" and spectatorship in general, that this "was to mean that of the two types into which Yeats divides artists, those who, like Blake, celebrate their own immediate share in the energy that 'is eternal delight,' and those who, like Keats, give us a poignant sense of being separated from what they present, James belonged to the latter."

It is true that James himself was much preoccupied with the whole matter of the definition of experience, in particular its dialectical relation to the dichotomy between action and contemplation. Furthermore, the preoccupation was a highly personal one. In this sense, Strether does embody some quintessential aspect of his author. The former is to learn retrospectively what James suggests his elders sensed prospectively about him when he was a child.

Speaking of his freedom to wander, to "dawdle and gape," he writes, "what I look back to as my infant license can only have had for its ground some timely conviction on the part of my elders that the only form of riot or revel ever known to me would be that of the visiting mind." In this same passage James, while speaking ruefully and compassionately of this "foredoomed" figure of himself as a small boy rubbing his "contemplative nose" against iron rails, nevertheless manages to transform that objective pauper into a subjective prince, an aristocrat of sensibility and the responding consciousness:

> He [the boy] might well have been even happier than he was. For there was the very pattern and measure of all he was to demand: just to *be* somewhere—almost anywhere would do—and somehow receive an impression or an accession, feel a relation or a vibration. . . . What it all appreciably gave him . . . [was] an education like another: feeling, as he has come to do more and more, that no education avails for the intelligence that doesn't stir some subjective passion, and that on the other hand almost anything that does so act is largely educative.
>
> (*A Small Boy and Others*)

The notion that the wealth of response and the sense of personal deprivation are somehow a function of each other is a continuous motif in James's work. In Strether's case, for example, things (such as Maria Gostrey's red velvet throat band) becomes precious and are in fact noticed to begin with because they symbolize all that he has ever yearned for and what he can never have. To have "lived" for Strether would have been to be in some state of possession in relation to the objects that pass before his eye: objects noticed by him in the first place because they stir his senses and because of their suggestibility. The human mind is, for James, by definition a haunted mind.

The haunting, furthermore, was implicit for him in the nature of consciousness, as the mode by which we both encounter life and are detached from it. For James, "experience" had two meanings, which themselves stand in an analogical relation to this opposition in the make-up of consciousness. On the one hand, experience meant action: the effective imposition of one's will upon the external world, participation, mastery; on the other, it means *re*action, a response of the mind, "a mark made on the intelligence," contemplation, passivity.

The first was something James could not imagine for himself. One of his earliest impressions, as we have seen, was that for him these two ways of being in the world were mutually exclusive. By a feat of intelligence that did not quite satisfy his yearning to be "other" than he was (other than contemplative), he transformed the latter definition into the one delineating the superior mode of being. Finally, experience wasn't experience unless it stirred that "vibration" and anything that did so—a mere act of seeing—qualified. But the other notion lingered in his imagination. One of the consequences of this was his art itself, in particular its central preoccupations, which are with the nature of consciousness as the "vibrating" recipient of impressions from the external world; its method, which is the imitation of precisely that process; and its forms, which are analogues for the capacity of the responding mind to shape its impressions, to create an architecture for them.

His characters repeat the process their author engages in: they construct imaginary worlds with their "visiting" minds, worlds that are the objectification of their desires but that are also unreal and doomed to collapse when brought into conjunction with the "facts." The facts are always that things are different from what a given character had wanted. The basic pattern of James's work is the creation and collapse of the fiction, its failure.

On another level, his sense of separation from life in its more energetic forms reflects itself in a continual yearning not for reality but for a kind of Marvellian paradise where peaches thrust themselves into his hands. He pines, that is, for an impossible and idyllic kind of gratification, yet when he reaches out in hunger he tastes only ashes. Between these two extremes he is characteristically unable to find peace. We have remarked earlier upon the essential ambivalence that lies at the center of his vision of life, and upon its typical embodiment in a dramatic situation that takes the form of a dilemma in which the actor is faced with a choice—but a choice that he tries not to make—between equally desirable goods on the one hand and equally undesirable ills on the other. Kate Croy, Milly Theale, and Maggie Verver all reject the premise that they must choose between one good and another: they try for everything. Milly looks down from the cliff, and Susan Stringham watching her wonders rhetorically if she is choosing among the kingdoms of the earth or if she wants them all. Kate, as we have seen [elsewhere], refuses to have Densher without a fortune or a fortune without Densher. And Maggie Verver tries to hold her husband to one breast and her father to the other. Strether, too, refuses to choose or to make a compromise between the set of possibilities represented by Europe and the set represented by America. Very much like Milly, through the process of self-deception, he at first clings to the belief that he can have the best (and none of the worst) of both worlds; then, undeluded, he renounces both. Strether, too, turns his face to the wall.

Nobody in James, hero or villain, ever gets what he wants. Or, if by some chance he gets what he thinks he wants, it has turned to poison. So Kate gets her fortune but finds that because of it she has lost her man. So Maggie keeps her husband but finds that she cannot look into his eyes because of the dread of seeing in them what she has done: to him, to Charlotte, to her father, to herself. In spite of the greed, the hunger, the so-obvious yearning for gratification that characterize the Jamesian actor, the inevitable outcome of events is frustration, pain, loss. James, concerned as he is with the destruction and collapse of the fiction, has essentially a negative rather than a tragic imagination.

In spite of his fundamental affinities with Hawthorne, he is in this respect closer to Poe, just as he is closer to Joyce and the early Eliot than to Lawrence, Faulkner, or Hemingway. Each of the latter has some version of a positive vision, a dialectic of salvation: Hemingway's ethos of the bull ring and rules of the game; Lawrence's prototype of blood and lust; Faulkner's process of sacrificial expiation and his celebration of the virtue of endurance. James has no such vision, nothing even remotely resembling it. Like Joyce, he portrays a pervasive emotional and spiritual paralysis, but he does not share Joyce's avowed visionary moral purpose in so doing. James's interests is in drama, not in persuasion.

This must be granted him. There exists no aesthetic basis for insisting that a writer feel and write "positively," or with tragic grandeur. We should grant the writer his donnée, as James said. From that point on what we can do is make the effort to articulate, with reasonable dispassion, the nature and various literary effects of the artist's symbolic world and the manner in which it is presented.

One of the main traits of James's symbolic world is indirection: of thought, speech, behavior, and feeling. It manifests itself in part in the persistent, almost ritualistic use of social masks and deceptive appearances, upon the uncovering of which so much of his ironic effect depends. Typically, the closest "friend" (Madame Merle, Kate Croy), unmasked, is the deadliest enemy; the "faithful" husband or lover in fact deeply attached to someone else; the affectionate mother (Mrs. Brooks, Charlotte Verver) the most ruthless sexual rival. In these kinds of oppositions and reversals, and in the starkness of the conflict, the agony of betrayal so near to home, there is something reminiscent of the "ghastly premises," as Nietzsche characterizes them, lurking in the plot of classical tragedy.

The habit of indirection, of circuitous, disguised, or evasive action, also manifests itself in a pronounced preference for various forms of "infantile" sexuality. James's success in dealing with such themes as homosexuality, child-contamination, and so on seems to depend upon his degree of conscious awareness, hence control of his theme and its implications. In *The Bostonians,* for example, James is fully in charge—at least of these aspects—and we are given a deliberate and compelling study of Olive Chancellor's lesbianism and its ramifications in the larger society of female Boston reformers. But in *The Portrait of a Lady,* where the issues of freedom, choice, and responsibility predominate, there is a strange lapse, a failure of connection between certain aspects of Isabel's private experience and these larger issues. Her narcissism, her frigidity, and the profound sexual terror she exhibits when Goodwood succeeds in arousing her remain undealt with, unrelated to the philosophical and moral motifs of the novel, yet the relation is in fact integral if not crucial. But because it is avoided by James, the ending of the book, Isabel's "inexplicable" decision to return to Osmond, is unsatisfactory and disturbing. The ostensible explanations offered: that she has made Pansy a promise; that she has made her own bed (so to speak) and will lie in it; that it is part of the meaning and nature of human responsibility to face the consequences of one's own choices, simply fail to be convincing in view of what seems a return to spiritual destitution. It is true that we do not *know* that Isabel might not find within herself enough strength to deal with Osmond, but, if so, we have to take her ability on faith. Furthermore, even if she were able to, it is hard to see, given his character, how the game could be worth the candle. But whether or not James intended to persuade us that it would be, the book still leaves unresolved the connections it raises between sex and morality. It is made very clear in the novel that she is afraid of Goodwood's sexuality, and her decision to return to Osmond is not definite until after the scene when Caspar kisses her in the garden. Whatever James's conscious intentions, the effect is to suggest a connection between these two things. James's evasion of the implications here is one of the few lapses in an otherwise superb novel. The result makes Isabel's collapse seem total and pointless; it becomes an immersion in futility, an apparent loss of will, of courage, of integrity. It is *this* that disagrees, as Strether would put it, with our spiritual stomach; not the suffering, but the banality on which it is based, the absurdity of its cause.

Such collapses of a character's will occur in James occasionally irrespective of any relationship they may have to sexual motifs per se. At times he was simply compelled by the pathos of the suffering, passive figure who (yearningly) renounces life, lets himself be wounded, crushed, or almost absorbed by someone else's will. He took a stand against this tendency in himself (when he complained, for example, that his hero Roderick Hudson had too much of the "principle of collapse") on the grounds that it involved a diminution of dramatic intensity and interest; to achieve these, he felt, there must be some provision for resistance and opposition of the central character to his fate: he (or she) might still be doomed, but not without a struggle.

However one characterizes what I have called James's negative imagination—as a tendency toward renunciation, evasion, indirection, or passive capitulation—it must be examined in terms of its literary effects. There has been an unfortunate tendency all along on the part of James's critics to drag his soul before the rostrum and sit in judgment of it, as if *that* were the issue: There is "no indication that he was capable of love"; he has "let his moral taste slip into abeyance"; "The relation between deficiency of this order [a deficiency in vitality] and the kind of moral unsatisfactoriness that we have observed in *The Golden Bowl* should be fairly plain." What, one wonders, would these critics have to say about the "moral sense" of the author of *Madame Bovary* or of *Troilus and Cressida* or, in relation to "vitality," of *Tamburlaine*?

As we pointed out [elsewhere], it is perfectly true that qualities like "energy directly exhibited" (as James described Tolstoy's work) are not characteristic of James's art. He was primarily interested in certain effects to be achieved by depicting the refraction of reality through the media of several consciousnesses, by radical experiments in architectonics, and by creating a luminous, sensuously metaphorical texture in his works. The "passivity" of certain of his characters is only one of many factors leading to a certain lustrously disembodied quality that his work sometimes has: much of his art has the effect of dividing our responses and preventing our "full" engagement with the fate—as such—of the characters. The interest is abstract, detached, intellectual rather than directly involved and felt. In some instances, in "The Beast in the Jungle" or in much of *The Golden Bowl,* for example, we may find ourselves more responsive to the patterning of events, the formal interplay of ironic reversal, or (in the novel) the richness of texture, than to the actual persons whom the events concern.

Passivity as such is much commoner in his male characters than in his female ones: what activity and vitality there are to be found in his fiction are in fact limited almost exclusively to the women characters. The number of "aggressive" males he depicts can be counted on the fingers of one hand, and they (Caspar Goodwood, Gloriani) are minor actors, functioning mainly as foils for a Gilbert Osmond or Lambert Strether. But the number of aggressive females is considerable: there is scarcely a novel in which the extreme weight of possibility and responsibility is not placed on the women, for good or ill. They are simply all over the place: doves and pantheresses, cool icebergs in some northern sea, Brittanias of the Marketplace and ladies. James's fictional world is dominated by females. "She wanted, Susan Shepherd," Merton reflects, "then, as appeared, the same thing Kate wanted. . . . Then Mrs. Lowder wanted, by so odd an evolution of her exuberance, exactly what each of the others did; and he was between them all, he was in the midst. . . . He was glad there was no male witness; it was a circle of petticoats; he shouldn't have liked a man to see him." Then, after Milly's death, in the presence of Sir Luke, he reflects again, "It was just by being a man of the world and by knowing life, by feeling the real, that Sir Luke did him good. There had been, in all the case, too many women. A man's sense of it, another man's, changed the air." In *The Golden Bowl,* the whole struggle is between Maggie and Charlotte: for possession, for dominance, for victory. The men await the will of their mates and the outcome of the battle for the prize male; for that is what it is, a story of two women fighting for the same man. The man prefers one, but it is the women who make the decision. The society in all three of the last novels, as well as in a number of the earlier ones, is a matriarchy.

The Ambassadors is especially interesting in this respect, for it is the only novel that explicitly articulates the masculine-feminine opposition into contrasting social structures. Even in *The Bostonians*, which deals with the relation between private and public life and has for its theme a battle to the death between the sexes, the only *society* as such is female. But in *The Ambassadors* we have a deliberate delineation of both a matriarchy and a patriarchy: the former the America of the invisible Mrs. Newsome and her husband, the latter the Europe of the invisible Compte de Vionnet and his wife. When the second group of ambassadors, Sally, Jim, and Mamie Pocock, come from America to accomplish the mission Strether has failed in, he begins to grasp that Jim's function is only decorative:

> Jim in fact, he presently made up his mind, was individ-ually out of it; Jim didn't care; Jim hadn't come out either for Chad or for him; Jim in short left the moral side to Sally and indeed simply availed himself now, for the sense of recreation, of the fact that he left almost everything to Sally. He was nothing compared to Sally, and not so much by reason of Sally's temper and will as by that of her more developed type and greater acquaintance with the world. He . . . confessed, as he sat there with Strether, that he felt his type hang far in the rear of his wife's and still further, if possible, in the rear of his sister's. Their types, he well knew, were recognised and acclaimed; whereas the most a leading Woollett business-man could hope to achieve socially, and for that matter industrially, was a certain freedom to play into this general glamour. . . .
>
> Pocock was normally and consentingly though not quite wittingly out of the question. It was despite his being normal; it was despite his being cheerful; it was despite his being a leading Woollett business-man. . . . He seemed to say that there was a whole side of life on which the perfectly usual *was* for leading Woollett business-men to be out of the question. . . . Strether's imagination, as always, worked, and he asked himself if this side of life were not somehow connected, for those who figured on it, with the fact of marriage. Would *his* relation to it, had he married ten years before, have become now the same as Pocock's? Might it even become the same should he marry in a few months?

> Should he ever know himself as much out of the question
> for Mrs. Newsome as Jim knew himself—in a dim way—
> for Mrs. Jim? . . .
>
> What . . . came home to him . . . at this hour, was that
> the society over there, that of which Sarah and Mamie—
> and, in a more eminent way, Mrs. Newsome herself—
> were specimens, was essentially a society of women, and
> that poor Jim wasn't in it.

Strether summarizes the role of the male in this woman-bound
society as one that exemplifies, simply, "failure of type," which
really means failure of individuality, not of generality or typicality.
"Small and fat and constantly facetious, straw-coloured and destitute
of marks, [Jim] would have been practically indistinguishable hadn't
his constant preference for light-grey clothes, for white hats, for very
big cigars and very little stories, done what it could for his identity."

The problem of self, the search for personal significance, is at
the very center of Strether's story: the novel has to be seen in part as
a comic quest for identity, and primarily sexual identity, even
though the quest is obscured under a number of layers of mist and is
articulated only indirectly in the book. In a way, *The Ambassadors* is
a refined parody of the motifs that Lionel Trilling discusses in his
introduction to *The Princess Casamassima:* the Young Man from the
Provinces and its cognate, the Sensitive Young Man. Like the first of
these, except that he is not young, Strether,

> equipped with . . . pride and intelligence . . . stands
> outside life and seeks to enter. This modern hero is
> connected with the tales of the folk. Usually his motive is
> the legendary one of setting out to seek his fortune, which
> is what the folktale says when it means that the hero is
> seeking himself. . . .
>
> It is the fate of the Young Man to move from an obscure
> position to one of considerable eminence, in Paris or
> London or St. Petersburg, to touch the life of the rulers of
> the earth. . . . He is confronted by situations whose
> meanings are dark to him.

And as with the second of these young men, it is Strether's "part
merely to be puzzled and hurt" by what he encounters. These legends,
and *The Ambassadors*, also contain a pastoral element, a contrast be-

tween innocence and corruption, a critique of "court" life. They are stories, too, of sexual initiation, the *rite de passage* into manhood.

The limits and the possibilities of Strether's quest are symbolized, as we have suggested, by the alternatives offered by the two contrasting civilizations and their respective styles of life and attitudes toward life, even their social and political structure. The book works toward two elaborate definitions of the significance that each culture has for Strether. What does he seek, what is his quest *for?* The whole book is a definition or articulation of this, through an intricate process of observation, perception, experience, and association on the part of the searcher, who is a man of divided inclinations.

To be a male in the America of Mrs. Newsome's Woollett, Massachusetts—at least a married male—is to be the second sex; to lack respect, responsibility, authority, and power; to be used for breeding and escort purposes but little else, in short, to lack personal identity. To be a male is to be "out of it," is to be not a type but rather, and precisely, a "failure of type."

Whereas the central phenomenon of Strether's European adventure is the very concept itself of "types," the hierarchical ordering of experience. Everything important that happens to him, everything that has any significance at all for him in Europe, is a function of some concrete embodiment of this concept or of something closely associated with it. As we have seen, it is intimate to the notion of taste, or an attitude toward *things* that is selective and qualitative, and to the experience itself of sensuous delight in those things that the imagination selects as worthy of delight. And who is best equipped to exercise the faculty of taste? Who but that type who most compels Strether's fancy, the man of the world. And what is the object best suited to delight his taste? What but that other great work of European art, the *femme du monde.* She, the woman who can look graceful with her elbows on the table, is the central image of desire in the novel, just as Mrs. Newsome (all "cold thought," all "moral pressure") is the central image of the repudiation of desire. Madame de Vionnet moves in a medium of privacy, peace, dignity, and style: the "ancient Paris" that Strether was always looking for and finds objectified by her surroundings. It

> was in the immemorial polish of the wide waxed staircase and in the fine *boiseries,* the medallions, mouldings, mirrors, great clear spaces, of the greyish-white salon into

which he had been shown. He seemed at the very outset to
see her in the midst of possessions not vulgarly numerous,
but hereditary cherished charming. . . . He had never
before, to his knowledge, had present to him relics, of any
special dignity, of a private order. . . . His attention took
them all tenderly into account. . . . Chad and Miss Gostrey had rummaged and purchased and picked up and
exchanged, sifting, selecting, comparing; whereas the
mistress of the scene before him, beautifully passive under
the spell of transmission—transmission from her father's
line, he quite made up his mind—had only received,
accepted and been quiet.

Her image is explicitly connected with the phenomena of
artistry, aristrocracy, patriarchy, and these in turn with her compelling sexuality: "At bottom of it all for him was the sense of her rare
unlikeness to the women he had known. . . . Everything in fine
made her immeasurably new, and nothing so new as the old house
and the old objects." Strether's Europe presents him, in other words,
with diverse realms of experience whose boundaries merge into one
another in phantasmagoric fashion, through the process of association, to form a complex symbolic pattern. There is a dreamlike
progression from the central concept of "type" through the related
concept of taste to the phenomenon of sensuous relish in the
immediate flux of experience, which in turn becomes associated in
Strether's mind with a kind of golden sensuality, paganism, and
uncorrupted sexuality. The last is of course his ardent puritan
delusion, his wishful belief in the "virtuous" nature of the attachment
between Chad and Madame de Vionnet: Strether wants to make a
Paradise of his Paris. His New England conscience is destined to be
overthrown twice, once when the delusion is shattered, again when
he is forced to acknowledge that virtue is not necessarily equatable
with chastity.

In the interim, however, the delusion serves its temporary
function of reconciling irreconcilable worlds, of removing the taint
of sin from the promise of masculinity. We have said earlier that all
of Strether's needs, wishes, and ambivalent response to both civilizations are focused upon Madame de Vionnet and Chad, and more
than anything else it is Chad's casual male dominance that attracts
and compels Strether. And here again, in the series of revolving

mirrors and shifting images by means of which Strether looks at Chad, we find the same progression from one realm of experience to another. Chad is "a gentleman," which is to say "a man of the world," "a young man marked out by women," "an irreducible young Pagan." There is no "failure of type" here, but a kind of lush abundance of alternative yet equivalent categories of identity in which being a gentleman is somehow the same as being a pagan. Chad is Strether's noble savage, his prefallen Adam; it is above all Chad's "romantic privilege" that he envies him, the privilege of having been young and happy in the charged air of Paris among the "delicate and appetising" effects of tone and tint, of having "the common, unattainable art of taking things as they come," of demonstrating in his person "some sense of power . . . something latent and beyond access, ominous and perhaps enviable."

And the society that has made this possible is a society in which prerogatives and authority are vested in the male. Madame de Vionnet's marriage was arranged for her; she had no option, no recourse. In return, Chad arranges the marriage of her daughter—at the very time when Woollett wishes him home not only for reasons of business but, more important, to "marry him off," and when Mrs. Newsome has taken the first steps in selecting his mate for him by sending Mamie Pocock along. Indeed, the striking contrast between the young girls produced by each culture is illuminating in this respect: Jeanne de Vionnet, *jeune fille,* delicate, charming, passive, perfectly obedient, and Mamie Pocock, already portly, mature, standing perpetually in the receiving line.

The great symbol of the male prerogative in this European civilization is the Catholic Church, that most organized of patriarchies. We have already seen that for Waymarsh the Church is emblematic of the intrinsic treachery of Europe: the "enemy," the "monster," the "multiplication of shibboleths . . . rank with feudalism," whose hierarchical ordering of the universe represents the grossest dangers to the free democratic spirit. The Church means "society" to Waymarsh and the "discrimination of types." We have seen the intricate associations that led from "mere discriminations about a pair of gloves" on Strether's part to fear of the "loss of his immortal soul": associations proceeding, once again, from the concept of "type" to that of taste, to enjoyment of sensuous particularity, from there to the hidden serpent lust buried in Europe's bosom; the American equation of sophistication with wickedness.

It is significant therefore to look at Strether's associations when he meets the great artist Gloriani in the company of ladies and gentlemen "in whose liberty to be as they were [Strether] was aware that he positively rejoiced." The scene, in a spacious garden attached to old noble houses with delicate and rare decorations, speaks to Strether "of survival, transmission, association, a strong indifferent persistent order." The open air in these conditions seems "a chamber of state," and he presently has "the sense of a great convent, a convent of missions, famous for he scarce knew what, a nursery of young priests, of scattered shade, of straight alleys and chapel-bells, that spread its mass in one quarter; he had the sense of names in the air, of ghosts at the windows, of signs and tokens, a whole range of expression, all about him, too thick for prompt discrimination."

Gloriani, Chad, Waymarsh, and little Bilham each in his way represents success to Strether, and each functions in the role of alter ego for him, but none so intensely as the great sculptor, "with his genius in his eyes, his manners on his lips, his long career behind him and his honours all round." During their brief encounter, with the sculptor's eyes holding his, Strether experiences a revelation about Gloriani that is at the same time a profound self-exposure; he is at a loss to know whether he has been told something or asked something. In fact, both things have occurred: each man has taken the measure of the other. The difficulty for poor Strether is his consciousness of how little there is in himself to be measured, either successful personal relationships or achievement in the affairs of men. But Gloriani represents both. Where Strether had dreamed in his youth of forming a relation with the higher culture and raising up the "temple of taste," Gloriani's accomplishments are realities, not broken dreams; with that "most special flare, unequalled, supreme, of the aesthetic torch, lighting that wondrous world for ever," he is "a dazzling prodigy of type," the great artist. And where "it was absolutely true" of Strether that "even after the close of the period of conscious detachment occupying the centre of his life, the grey middle desert of the two deaths, that of his wife and that, ten years later, of his boy—he had never taken any one anywhere," Gloriani is surrounded by *femmes du monde;* there is "deep human expertness in [his] charming smile—of, the terrible life behind it!"; he is "the glossy male tiger, magnificently marked."

This vision of Gloriani is the apotheosis of Strether's European adventure. The artist is the exalted image of the complex set of personal possibilities—ones, however, that only *might* have been, represented by Europe for Strether, who is reduced to murmuring helplessly after their encounter, "Oh, if everything had been different!" The whole novel, as has been mentioned, is an elaborate definition of what constitutes that "everything," but all the intricate associations making up the definition are condensed and fused in the figure of Gloriani: Strether's longing for release from both avoidance and caution (which is his definition of personal freedom) so that he might enjoy the thing of the moment, take things as they come, satiate his appetite for beautiful things, even smoke with a woman. The latter of course is a thinly disguised version of the male tiger's activities: one must always with Strether's remarks about himself read behind the obscuring veil dropped by his New England conscience. But no matter what the devious routes, mazes and metaphors, elaborate veneers of civilization, all the paths in this novel lead finally to the jungle (Strether's word). With whatever overlays of ambivalence, the ordeal of sexuality is *the* major theme of *The Ambassadors*.

This ambivalence is of course conscious, intentional: we are warned at the outset of the oddity of Strether's double nature; he is intended to be the embodiment of the reluctant puritan, hating his own "odious ascetic suspicion of any form of beauty," labeling with the word "failure" the general inability to enjoy that is one of Woollett's main characteristics, recognizing with an inward chill that Mrs. Newsome is "all cold thought" or "all moral pressure." The drama of the novel is meant to be a drama of self-division. Strether dips his toe, so to speak, in the unholy waters of Babylon but remains shivering, and peeping, on the bank while others take the plunge for him. This insistent yet somewhat shady, or voyeuristic, timorousness is typical of James's sensitive male protagonists and here is superbly faithful to the novel's study of the New England conscience and the American puritan temperament, one characteristic of which is precisely the combination of rectitude of behavior and lasciviousness of thought. It is a diabolic twosome, as Hawthorne knows, and shows so well in "The Minister's Black Veil," where the man of God imagines sin where none exists and himself becomes the profound emblem of righteous dirty-mindedness. Similarly, when in their initial interview, Chad denies that he is or ever was "entangled," Strether asks,

"Then what are you here for? What has kept you? . . . if you *have* been able to leave?"

It made Chad, after a stare, throw himself back. "Do you think one's kept only by women?" His surprise and his verbal emphasis rang out so clear in the still street that Strether winced till he remembered the safety of their English speech. "Is that," the young man demanded, "what they think at Woollett?" At the good faith in the question Strether had changed colour, feeling that, as he would have said, he had put his foot in it. He had appeared stupidly to misrepresent what they thought at Woollett; but before he had time to rectify Chad again was upon him. "I must say then you show a low mind."

It is of course what they think at Woollett, and there has been no misrepresentation except as Strether would feel, in the spirit of the thing: Woollett is after all indignant, not acquiescent, and the filth isn't their own imagining (he imagines): Chad *is* being kept by a woman. As indeed he is; Strether's ethical reeducation in Europe eventually leads him to the point where he ceases to make the automatic equation between sex and sin, at least for others. But for himself the two sides of the dialectic remain unsynthesized, and the real end result of his adventures is to render America and Europe both unfit abodes for his soul. Furthermore, such an outcome is absolutely characteristic of James. It is intrinsic to his imaginative vision of things to see the world as rent asunder, with half its goods on the left hand of God, half on the right, and no passage in between. But what is more uniquely Jamesian, since most serious literature deals in dichotomy, opposition, and paradox, is that the negative sides of his dilemmas are the ones that speak the loudest and hold final sway. This is true of him beyond logic, and so consistently true that it amounts to a compulsive orientation to existence; at the very least a repetitive stance of negation. For there is nothing inherent in the logical structure of a dilemma that makes defeat a necessity. There is only one necessity in a genuine dilemma, and that is compromise, or the sacrifice of what one hopes is the lesser good for the sake of keeping the greater. And it is just this necessity that the Jamesian character typically rejects. Strether, Kate Croy, Milly Theale, and even Merton Densher, each in his way, all want the best of both possible worlds, the best, or nothing. There is a latent but insistent streak of romanticism in James that manifests itself in this character-istic rejection of the limitations that are inherent in every human situation. It has long been recognized by critics, and usually with considerable irritation, that James releases his characters from the ordinary burdens of economic necessity (Adam Verver is a multi-millionaire, Isabel Archer is left a massive fortune in the first flush of her youth, Milly Theale is "the heiress of all the ages," and even Strether has "enough" that it is a matter of concern to him to select an heir), but it has been less well recognized that he endows these same characters with the impulse to be free from all necessity and restriction. When Madame Merle tells Isabel that the clothes one wears, the books one reads, the company one keeps are all the palpable expressions of one's self, Isabel demurs:

> "I don't agree with you. I think just the other way. I don't know whether I succeed in expressing myself, but I know that nothing else expresses me. Nothing that belongs to me is any measure of me; everything's on the contrary a limit, a barrier, and a perfectly arbitrary one. Certainly the clothes which, as you say, I choose to wear, don't express me; and heaven forbid they should!"
>
> "You dress very well," Madame Merle lightly inter-posed.
>
> "Possibly; but I don't care to be judged by that. My clothes may express the dressmaker, but they don't express me. To begin with it's not my own choice that I wear them; they're imposed upon me by society."
>
> "Should you prefer to go without them?" Madame Merle enquired in a tone which virtually terminated the discussion.
>
> (*The Portrait of a Lady*)

But Isabel is not the only rebel against barriers; Kate, Milly, Charlotte, Maggie, even poor hesitant Strether all have immortal longings, all resist to the last degree of their energy the acknowl-edgement that the world either is not, or cannot be made into, the image of their own desires. The pattern that follows the acknowl-edgement is that of renunciation if not collapse: Isabel returning to Osmond; Strether a permanent exile from both landscapes of his soul; Charlotte whimpering like a wounded animal, being led to America by an "invisible noose," a silken cord in her husband's hand; the Prince docile and impotent awaiting his wife's pleasure; Milly turning her face to the wall.

James's own definition of romance centers precisely upon this phenomenon of the limits, the conditions that attend experience.

> The only *general* attribute of projected romance that I can see, the only one that fits all its cases, is the fact of the kind of experience with which it deals—experience liberated, so to speak; experience disengaged, disembroiled, disencumbered, exempt from the conditions that we usually know to attach to it and, if we wish so to put the matter, drag upon it, and operating in a medium which relieves it . . . of the inconvenience of a *related,* a measurable state, a state subject to all our vulgar communities. . . . The balloon of experience is in fact of course tied to the earth, and under that necessity we swing, thanks to a rope of considerable length, in the more or less commodious car of the imagination; but it is by the rope we know where we are, and from the moment that cable is cut we are at large and unrelated; we only swing apart from the globe—though remaining as exhilarated, naturally, as we like, especially when all goes well. The art of the romancer is, "for the fun of it," insidiously to cut the cable, to cut it without our detecting him.
>
> (*The Art of the Novel*)

Isabel would understand her creator's metaphor: her own imagery of life is not unlike it.

> "Do you know where you are going, Isabel Archer?"
>
> "Just now I'm going to bed," said Isabel with persistent frivolity.
>
> "Do you know where you're drifting?" Henrietta pursued. . . .
>
> "No, I haven't the least idea, and I find it very pleasant not to know. A swift carriage, of a dark night, rattling with four horses over roads that one can't see—that's my idea of happiness."
>
> (*The Portrait of a Lady*)

Even the unusual severity of the conditions that in fact attend the lives and possibilities of these characters (what after all does one do when one discovers that one's husband and stepmother are lovers? or that a mortal illness can only be interrupted by falling in love?) is itself a romantic phenomenon, paradoxical though it may seem. For the very severity is an idealization: not so much improbable as extraordinary and uncontrolled, as James would say, "by our general sense of 'the way things happen.'" The tests are severer, the pain intenser and at the same time more "exalted" than we would ordinarily expect to find even in the difficult aspects of our everyday lives. So that what we discover again and again in the dramatic situation of these novels is a group of characters whose unusually strong impulse to reject restriction must act itself out in a situation that is unusually restricted. The process of avoiding a choice between one set of possibilities and another, in other words of compromising, may vary from person to person—Strether and Milly deceive themselves about the nature of the reality around them, Densher deludes himself about the nature of his own actions, Kate simply denies that a dilemma exists—but the essential phenomenon is the same in each case and consists of a refusal to make peace with reality, to accept or even to acknowledge the limitations that are a part of every human situation. And this is a characteristic of "hero" and "villain" alike in James's world: both types are overreachers. The difference between them is in the nature of their illusions, not in their fundamental denial of reality. Thus the characteristic illusion of the Jamesian villain is that he may with impunity get what he wants simply by taking it regardless of who else may suffer in the process, and the characteristic illusion of the hero is that no one would ever harm him for the sake of gain, or for any other reason. Both types have an extraordinary faith in appearances: the latter typically believes that appearances are all there is, that the world *is* the way it seems, the former that appearances are all that matters, that immunity from retribution is automatically achieved by protective coloration. Thus the great deceivers in the novels—Madame Merle and Osmond, Kate and Densher and Aunt Maud, Chad and Madame de Vionnet, Charlotte and the Prince—all take pains to keep their social masks flawless: polished, perfect and automatic. The golden bowl has a crack, a flaw, but great care is taken by the author to make it clear to us that the flaw is *imperceptible,* invisible to the naked, certainly to the untrained, inexpert eye.

The basic pattern of all these novels is the same; it consists of the gradual undeception of protagonist and antagonist alike, but always after irrevocable harm has been done. The same painful lessons are learned too late again and again by both camps on the battlefield. Kate's final word to her lover, and the note on which the book closes, is "we shall never be again as we were!"; and Madame de Vionnet's final interview with Strether wrings from her the admission that she has made a change in his life:

> "I've upset everything in your mind as well; in your sense of—what shall I call it?—all the decencies and possibilities. It gives me a kind of detestation . . . of everything, of life. . . .
>
> What I hate is myself—when I think that one has to take so much, to be happy, out of the lives of others, and that one isn't happy even then. One does it to cheat one's self and to stop one's mouth—but that's only at the best for a little. The wretched self is always there, always making one somehow a fresh anxiety. What it comes to is that it's not, that it's never, a happiness, any happiness at all, to *take*. The only safe thing is to give. It's what plays you least false."

But if there is never any happiness in taking, neither is there in the determined pretense that takers are absent from the world. James's victims share the burden of responsibility with their victimizers, and the events of the novels must be seen as a kind of cooperative venture in pain. The "guilt" of Isabel, Milly, Strether, and Maggie is a wilful blindness, a staggering self-deception based upon wishful thinking. The victims in each case wish to believe in the appearance put forth by those who practice upon them; their cases are complementary, and the responsibility is divided. James's finest talent in a way is for seeing what will not work. He is the most unsentimental of our great romanticists.

Strether's Curious "Second Wind": Imagination and Experience in *The Ambassadors*

Philip M. Weinstein

> *"One of the pair," I said, "has to pay for the other. What ensues is a miracle, and miracles are expensive. What's a greater one than to have your youth twice over? It's a second wind, another 'go'—which isn't the sort of thing life mostly treats us to."*
>
> The Sacred Fount

> *What happened all the while, I conceive, was that I imagined things . . . wholly other than as they were, and so carried on in the midst of the actual ones an existence that somehow floated and saved me even while cutting me off from any degree of direct performance, in fact from any degree of direct participation, at all.*
>
> A Small Boy and Others

> *Perception is not whimsical, but fatal.*
EMERSON, "Self-Reliance"

Unlike *The Sacred Fount*, *The Ambassadors* fully merits the critical attention it has received. Whether it be his best novel or, as Warner Berthoff puts it, "only his most perfectly charming," it has elicited brilliant commentary from Percy Lubbock in 1921 to Sallie Sears in 1968. Their work, as well as that of Oscar Cargill, Laurence Holland, Christof Wegelin, Robert Garis, Tony Tanner, and Richard Poirier, has proved particularly helpful, but the book remains inexhaustible. The pages that follow are not so much a challenge to

---

From *Henry James and the Requirements of the Imagination*. © 1971 by the President and Fellows of Harvard College. Harvard University Press, 1971.

the above critics as a fleshed-out reading of the particular drama—located among the many dramas indicated by others—that *The Ambassadors* seems most interestingly to embody: the fundamental relation between a character's imagination, the experience he seeks to interpret, and the experience he finally undergoes.

As observer-actor, Strether represents the mature development of a kind of character James first seriously sketched in Rowland Mallet. The earlier character, possessed of a "moral and aesthetic curiosity" (*Roderick Hudson*), ambiguously connected with the drama of a younger man toward whom he is expected to act as a moral guardian of sorts, and finally stranded on his return to America, is an unmistakable precursor of Strether. And we can measure a certain direction of James's development by the difference in our response to the two men.

In the early novel James seems undecided as to his primary subject, vacillating in emphasis between Roderick's adventures and Rowland's perception of them. As I suggested in my first chapter, this dilemma serves as a turning point in the development of James's characteristic view of experience. The Roderick figure continues in Newman, in the early Isabel, in Basil Ransom, in Paul Muniment, and in Chad. But the figure who means most for James's development, and who leads to Ralph Touchett and to the Isabel of book 2, to Hyacinth, Fleda Vetch, Maisie, Nanda, the narrator of *The Sacred Fount,* Strether, Milly, and Maggie, is surely the sensitive and observant, the passive and imaginative Rowland Mallet.

In *The Ambassadors* the main subject—Strether—is developed with a massive fullness unmatched elsewhere in James's fiction. Every conversation, every observed, imagined, or remembered relationship has an interest both in itself and as it bears on Strether's fate. Although the consciousness of Rowland Mallet was the point of view for telling Roderick's story in the earlier novel, Rowland himself remained at times only vaguely implicated in the sculptor's life, and the comparative thinness of *Roderick Hudson* derives from James's failure to establish vividly either the drama or Roderick's adventures or the intensity of Rowland's relation to them.

In his next important novels James seems to have combined (in Christopher Newman and in Isabel Archer) the roles of actor and observer that were fragmented in *Roderick Hudson;* Isabel looms as large in her novel as Strether does in his. But, although one sees mainly from her perspective, the contours of her mind and the precise nature of her emotional responses are rarely so intimately known as Strether's are. Isabel remains a magnificent creation but often inscrutable, rendered somehow from the outside; Strether, despite James's poised, complex stance toward him, is presented more tenderly and more nearly from within.

This is a loosely expressed point, but one with important ramifications. Because we are relatively farther from Isabel's mind than from Strether's, and because the world she encounters is seen by us as immediately other than the way she sees it, we develop a more detached and critical attitude toward her romance. In other words, by not giving us, in *The Ambassadors,* a scene, like the early, clarifying one between Gilbert Osmond and Madame Merle, by refracting everything through Strether's consciousness, James prevents us from incisively "placing" Strether's errors as we can place Isabel's. Consequently, Strether's imagination plays a broader and more sympathetic role than Isabel's in shaping the reader's response. This change in emphasis has important implications: first, it accounts for the richly embroidered, playful prose of *The Ambassadors*; more important, however, it underlies our final feeling that, while Isabel has been cheated, Strether *has* somehow had his experience. By keeping us gently critical of Isabel's imagination and then concluding her experience with loss and disillusionment, James makes us respond to the ending of *The Portrait of a Lady* as tragic.

But the conclusion of *The Ambassadors* occasions in us no such somber response. Unlike Isabel, Strether has largely and consciously limited his goal to the realm of the imagination alone: when other realms fail and Strether departs with nothing else, he has at least (or supremely) had his imaginative adventure. Placed within his mind, we feel no tragic loss; we have, in a sense, undergone his experience with him, an experience impaired but not, like Isabel's, bitterly mocked by the losses and renunciations with which the novel ends. These differences should become clearer in my analysis of *The Ambassadors*.

Among the protagonists who precede Strether, Maisie and the narrator of *The Sacred Fount,* do not "act," as Isabel does, on the grand scale. Like Rowland and Ralph Touchett, they are primarily engaged in seeing, but the emphasis in their stories shifts increasingly from what they see to how they see. Moreover, they become central rather than peripheral characters. To oversimplify, one might say that *The Sacred Fount* is comparable to *Roderick Hudson* without

Roderick or to *The Portrait of a Lady* projected from Ralph Touchett's point of view, without the solid presence of Isabel Archer and her well-defined drama. In his quest for perception, Strether of course resembles Maisie and the narrator of *The Sacred Fount*. But *The Ambassadors*—unlike the two shorter novels that precede it and harking back to the novels of the eighties—reasserts a major stress on the world being perceived. Put more concretely, the physical and human worlds of Paris, of Chad and Madame de Vionnet, are rendered by James as something real, something important in their own right, not primarily as an index to Strether's mind. And yet the triumph of the novel is that Strether's mind is portrayed, through its contact with these worlds, with a more impressive delicacy and intensity than James achieves in the creation of either Maisie or the narrator of the *Fount*.

Strether embodies characteristics and concerns that have been common to James's earlier heroes from Rowland to the narrator of *The Sacred Fount*. Moreover, in the spectrum of life confronted by Strether, *The Ambassadors* presents a synthesis of the two major kinds of experience that this study has been exploring. To encounter the world of European civilization, in *Roderick Hudson* and in *The Portrait of a Lady,* is one of the deepest desires of the protagonist; for Isabel Archer, it is paramount. *What Maisie Knew* and *The Sacred Fount* project, however, a range of experience both narrower and, in a sense, more basic. Passive and psychically isolated, Maisie and the narrator cannot afford the "luxury" of Isabel's adventures. Up to their necks in an epistemological morass, they are not concerned with the refinement that comes from an encounter with the "great world." Rather, they struggle at the elementary level of meaning itself; their attempt is simply to make some sense of the world of passion and intimacy that surrounds them. In *The Ambassadors,* through Strether's adventure, as later in *The Golden Bowl,* the odyssey into European civilization and the encounter with sexual intimacy merge into a comprehensive rendering of the Jamesian vision of human experience.

Finally, because of his age, his past, his temperament, and his peculiar errand, Strether's experience of the European world comes to him largely as shaped by his imagination. To examine his drama in Paris is to explore the interplay between the energies of one of James's most imaginative heroes and the outside world of the largest, most typical experience. As justification for such a detailed analysis of this novel, I suggest that the shape of Strether's drama is indeed the figure in the carpet of James's work, the major trope with which this study has been concerned.

> Live all you can, it's a mistake, not to. It doesn't so much matter what you do in particular, so long as you have your life. If you haven't had that what *have* you had?

> That, you see, is my only logic. Not, out of the whole affair, to have got anything for myself.

Between these two speeches—each pointing to an opposite extreme—one can locate Strether's approach toward experience. Overwhelmed by the magnificent pageant in Gloriani's garden, Strether recalls the failed occasions and accumulated mediocrity of his own life, and he passionately urges little Bilham not to make the same mistake. Although couched in deterministic phrases (not quoted here) that acknowledge that it is too late for himself, Strether's outburst is a paean to freedom and self-development, an exhortation to live life to the fullest. It contrasts vividly with the reflective, fastidious tone of the later speech in which Strether justifies self-denial as the only possible conclusion to his experience. This chapter attempts to relate these contradictory speeches: to qualify the first one and, as regards the second, to suggest what, after all, Strether does get for himself "out of the whole affair."

> That he was prepared to be vague to Waymarsh about the hour of the ship's touching, and that he both wanted extremely to see him and enjoyed extremely the duration of delay—these things, it is to be conceived, were early signs in him that his relation to his actual errand might prove none of the simplest. He was burdened, poor Strether—it had better be confessed at the outset—with the oddity of a double consciousness. There was detachment in his zeal and curiosity in his indifference.

Some light on Strether's ambiguous position is cast by this passage, which occurs on the third page of the narrative and caps a series of uneasy meditations that began with the novel's opening phrase: "Strether's first question." Strether is constantly (and delightfully) asking questions and having misgivings throughout his adventure. The uneasiness derives from his "oddity of a double consciousness," and, in his conflicting desires to experience Europe and to remain true to his moral categories, he exhibits a duality that echoes Isabel Archer's "mixture of curiosity and fastidiousness, of vivacity and indifference."

On the one hand, Strether has been assigned the specific task of bringing Chad back to the fold, and any enjoyment in the interim is liable to undermine his precarious authority. Thus his trip to Europe can be seen as an uncomfortable, sacrificial ordeal undergone for Mrs. Newsome; and Marie Gostrey, seeing it at first in these terms, remarks: "You'd do at any rate this [go to Europe for Mrs. Newsome and Sarah], and the 'anything' they'd do is represented by their *making* you do it." Of course Strether knows (and this is what makes him uneasy) that they are not "making" him do anything, that, furtively and for a long time, he has yearned to return to Europe and redeem his "promise" made thirty years ago. When Maria concludes that he is not "enjoying it" so much as he ought, she is unaware of the complexity of motives and characteristics in Strether that make him capable of enjoying Europe less than he wants to and more than he thinks he ought to.

The commitment to Woollett is a complex one, composed of admiration and gratitude toward Mrs. Newsome—she is, after all, the only person who has acted toward him in a generous way since the death of his own family—but composed also of material promises, of a future full of peace and security for his old age. Underlying both of these aspects of the Woollett commitment are certain buried moral premises and attitudes toward experience that become resurrected and transformed during the course of his adventure in Paris.

Opposing the commitment to Mrs. Newsome, on the other hand, is a concealed but profound desire to make the most of his European experience. Strether has always been vaguely aware of his personal failure, and the return to Paris makes this awareness throb: "The special spring that had constantly played for him the day before was the recognition—frequent enough to surprise him—of the promises to himself that he had after his other visit never kept." Moreover, the "consciousness of personal freedom as he hadn't known for years" implies that Mrs. Newsome and the marriage that awaits his return home are already viewed with mixed feelings. Freedom and experience—the dream of a certain fulfillment—are felt by Strether in Paris rather than anticipated as rewards attending his homecoming: it both surprises and embarrasses him to note how much his being in Paris figures for him as an escape. The betrayal of his youthful promises made years ago in Paris is further compounded by a later "betrayal" of his own son; through unrestrained grief for his wife's untimely death, Strether grew estranged from his son, and the latter's death has left Strether scarred with feelings of guilt.

The sense of personal failure, the ambiguous feeling toward his Woollett future, and the guilt incurred from "betraying" his own son render him especially vulnerable to Chad's Parisian drama. Adoption of Chad's point of view will symbolically redeem Strether's earlier failure to profit by Paris; to befriend Chad is, again symbolically, to atone for his failure toward his dead son. These reasons for Strether's susceptibility are sufficient to account for his squirming throughout the novel; anchored in his cultural inheritance and his own past, they act as a background for his European adventure. What brings them into play and gives unique shape to Strether's experience in Paris, what quickens both his enjoyment and his self-criticism, is his faculty of appreciation, his ripening imagination.

Strether embarks for Europe with what may be called a Woollett imagination; he and the town's moral emblem—Mrs. Newsome—see Chad the same way. They both have imagined "horrors," and he is consequently amazed by Maria Gostrey's exclamation, "She may be charming—his life!"

> "Charming?"—Strether stared before him. "She's base, venal—out of the streets."
> "I see. And he—?"
> "Chad, wretched boy?"
> "Of what type and temper is he?" she went on as Strether had lapsed.
> "Well—the obstinate." It was as if for a moment he had been going to say more and had then controlled himself.
> That was scarce what she wished. "Do you like him?"
> This time he was prompt. "No. How can I?"
> "Do you mean because of your being so saddled with him?"
> "I'm thinking of his mother," said Strether after a moment. "He has darkened her admirable life." He spoke with austerity.

"Intensity with ignorance," Maria's later phrase for Mrs. Newsome's imagination, aptly describes Strether's own in this scene. Trying to elicit a concrete description of the "problem," Maria succeeds in drawing from Strether only abstract phrases of moral condemnation. His codified point of view stymies the conversation and blocks the passage of any information other than his own righteous disapproval. Stung by what he can only consider the perversity of Maria's questions, Strether is unable detachedly to consider Chad as a complex human being ("No. How *can* I?"), and the consequent impoverishment of his perceptions is expressed by the clichés that creep into his conversation: "She's base, venal—out of the streets"; "Chad, wretched boy"; "He has darkened her admirable life." There are close-minded, dogmatic judgments, just the reverse of those marvelous exploratory conversations found elsewhere in James, which are punctuated by question marks and seek new information, rather than doctrinally elaborating old positions. Warned by his tone, Maria Gostrey cannot enlighten him. She has no choice but hypocrisy ("I see"), and Strether is saved from a fate of "splendid" isolation—like Waymarsh's—only through his ability to develop beyond this position.

The Woollett imagination in Strether expresses itself not only through clichés but also through the limited meanings he is able to attach to certain phrases: " '*Now* don't you see,' she [Maria] went on, 'why the boy doesn't come home? He's drowning his shame.' 'His shame? [Strether replies] What shame?' " The interchange rises effortlessly to a contrast between Puritan New England and aesthetic Paris. Maria posits the dubiously acquired Newsome fortune as the "shame" from which the finer-grained Chad is fleeing; while to Strether's imagination how one makes money is virtually outside moral categories, the obviously outrageous shame in the affair being Chad's corruption by a "base, venal" woman.

The richest example of an untutored imagination revealed through ignorance of what words may mean occurs in a colloquy with little Bilham: " 'He wants to be free. He isn't used, you see,' the young man explained in his lucid way, 'to being so good.' Strether hesitated. 'Then I may take it from you that he *is* good?' His companion matched his pause, but making it up with a quiet fulness. '*Do* take it from me.' " Strether then persists, "Why isn't he free if he's good?" to which, looking him "full in the face," little Bilham finally replies, "Because it's a virtuous attachment."

Strether's one-sided application of moral terms to an illicit sexual union leads him quite awry. If Chad is "good," he reasons, he must then be "free" and cannot be sexually involved. In little Bilham's view, however, freedom is incommensurate with such goodness, and this darker equation, while unknown to Strether, serves the reader as a qualification of the famous outburst in Gloriani's garden, for it unobtrusively prefigures the losses and renunciations—the "cost" of being "good"—with which the novel closes. Strether, however, is unaware of these complications; at this point "a virtuous attachment" is for his imagination, if not for little Bilham's, a simplifying rubric.

But once he has seen Chad, everything begins to alter, and the second "phase" of the journey of Strether's imagination commences with is appreciating to the full Chad's marvelous transformation: "Chad's case—whatever else of minor interest it might yield—was first and foremost a miracle almost monstrous. It was the alteration of the entire man, and was so signal an instant that nothing else, for the intelligent observer, could—*could* it?—signify." The extreme phrasing—"miracle almost monstrous," "entire man," "nothing else," "*could* it?"—conveys the wonder and possible excess of Strether's reaction. Moored for years to Woollett's horizons, his liberated imagination has, in the phrase used for Isabel Archer, "jumped out of the window." After a lifetime of inertia and mediocrity, now furtively seeking in Europe something he began thirty years before but failed to make good on, Strether is quick to see in Chad transcendent development, a man made over. It is a case of fatal perception; Strether *has* glimpsed something extraordinary, and later qualifications can only reduce his estimate of Chad without marring the beauty of his vision. The image of successful change and the apparent realization of his long-abandoned European ideal touch his own private desires too nearly to be relinquished. Chad moves Strether most deeply not as a substitute son but as the living embodiment of the youth he now realizes he never remotely had.

This growing fascination with youth lends a vivid allure to the silhouetted figure of little Bilham on the balcony:

> He was young too then, the gentleman up there—he was very young . . . there was youth in the surrender to the balcony, there was youth for Strether at this moment in everything but his own business; and Chad's thus pro-

nounced association with youth had given the next instant an extraordinary quick lift to the issue. The balcony, the distinguished front, testified suddenly, for Strether's fancy, to something that was up and up; they placed the whole case materially, and as by an admirable image, on a level that he found himself at the end of another moment rejoicing to think he might reach. . . . It came to pass before he moved that Waymarsh, and Waymarsh alone . . . struck him as the present alternative to the young man in the balcony. When he did move it was fairly to escape that alternative.

The passage exhibits the power of Strether's "fancy" to create a symbolic, "admirable image" from a natural situation, and Strether's climbing to the height of that balcony, like his later climbing those same four stories "for Chad's life," translates his imaginative vision into active experience, into gestures of personal commitment. As with Isabel, however, the gesture of self-assertion is also an "escape" from "alternatives" suddenly seen as intolerable.

In Gloriani's garden, where Parisian life is most before him, Strether understandably links the sculpture's charm with Chad's unfailing ease and, through that connection, with his own yearning: "Chad . . . was a kind of link for hopeless fancy, an implication of possibilities—oh if everything had been different!" At the end of the party the connection through memory between his abortive youth and Chad's achievement is complete: " 'Oh Chad!'—it was that rare youth he should have enjoyed being 'like.' " The implications of this connection are writ large in Strether's behavior in Paris and will be explored later. I am concerned here with the imaginative release it occasions in Strether, as is indicated in the following outburst to Maria Gostrey:

> I don't get drunk; I don't pursue the ladies; I don't spend money; I don't even write sonnets. But nevertheless I'm making up late for what I didn't have early. . . . It amuses me more than anything that has happened to me in all my life. They may say what they like—it's my surrender, it's my tribute, to youth. One puts that in where one can—it has come in somewhere, if only out of the lives, the conditions, the feelings of other persons. Chad gives me the sense of it, for all his grey hairs . . . and *she* does the

same, for all her marriageable daughter, her separated husband, her agitated history. Though they're young enough, my pair, I don't say they're . . . their *own* absolutely prime adolescence; for that has nothing to do with it. The point is that they're mine. Yes, they're my youth; since somehow at the right time nothing else ever was.

Madame de Vionnet, too, is part of his youth, and if his imaginative vision of Chad is shaped by the current of memory, what his imagination makes of her is even more strikingly a creation of his dormant ideals and desires. As with his encounter with Chad at the theater, Strether's first impression of Madame de Vionnet is too "massive" to be related in the present tense alone. "He was to feel," "our friend was to go over it afterwards again and again"— these fusions of the past and future tenses indicate how the sheer weight of Strether's impressions and the lavish care he devotes to them transcend the moment when they are made. While the vision of Chad summoned the memory of Strether's own past, Madame de Vionnet gradually comes symbolically to bridge for him an even greater number of years, to represent the historic beauty and continuity of French civilization.

His first impression, which a little disappoints his Woollett curiosity about the exotic, is of her "common humanity"; and he is puzzled that a woman so like his female acquaintances might possibly be Chad's lover. His imagination begins to embroider her traits, however, as he sees in her dignified apartment a hint of the ancient Paris, "some glory, some prosperity of the First Empire, some Napoleonic glamour, some dim lustre of the great legend." In formal dress she strikes his imagination as "some silver coin of the Renaissance" or "a goddess" or "sea-nymph waist-high in the summer surge. Above all she suggested to him the reflexion that the *femme du monde*—in these finest developments of the type—was, like Cleopatra in the play, indeed various and multifold."

Hints abound that Strether appreciates without coolly analyzing Madame de Vionnet, and the figures of the "goddess still partly engaged in a morning cloud" and the partly hidden "sea-nymph" delicately suggest the chaste boundaries of Strether's fertile imagination. When he sees her praying in Notre Dame, "she reminded our friend—since it was the way of nine tenths of his current impressions to act as recalls of things imagined—of some fine firm concentrated heroine of an old story." His imagination associates her with the heroines of Victor Hugo, finds her "romantic . . . far beyond what she could have guessed"; and he intuitively decides that "unassailably innocent was a relation that could make one of the parties to it so carry herself."

Such analogies from the world of art suffuse *The Ambassadors*. This one both echoes the London melodrama Strether witnessed with Maria (which corroborated his melodramatic vision of Chad's affair) and prefigures his identification of rural France with the never-attained Lambeint of his youth. Considering the novel in this light, Richard Poirier generalizes: "*The Ambassadors* offers remarkably beautiful instances of the hero's effort to transform the things he sees into visions, to detach them from time and from the demands of nature, and to give them the composition of *objets d'art*. The novel is about the cost and profit for such acts of imagination."

The most suggestive allusion is the one to Cleopatra, for it hints at both Madame de Vionnet's rich sexual vitality (which he ignores) and her inscrutable "mixture of lucidity and mystery. She fell in at moments with the theory about her he most cherished, and she seemed at others to blow it into air. She spoke now as if her art were all an innocence, and then again as if her innocence were all an art." Enchantingly beyond analysis, she exerts the same influence on Strether's imagination that Paris does, "a jewel brilliant and hard, in which parts were not to be discriminated nor differences comfortably marked. It twinkled and trembled and melted together, and what seemed all surface one moment seemed all depth the next." This mixture of appreciation and error in his vision of Madame de Vionnet characterizes the general attempt of his imagination to fathom the appearances that confront him. We might now measure how far he travels from his Woollett stereotypes, yet how distant he remains from Parisian sophistication.

When Strether marvels at the unexpected change in Chad after the encounter in the theater, Maria is impatient at his not having "seen" the female influence:

> She got up from her chair, at this, with a nearer approach than she had ever yet shown to dismay at his dimness. She even, fairly pausing for it, spoke with a shade of pity. "Guess!"

It was a shade, fairly, that brought a flush into his face; so that for a moment . . . their difference was between them. "You mean that just your hour with him told you so much of his story? Very good; I'm not such a fool, on my side, as that I don't understand you, or as that I didn't in some degree understand him. That he has done what he liked most isn't, among any of us, a matter the least in dispute. There's equally little question at this time of day of what it is he does like most. But I'm not talking," he reasonably explained, "of any mere wretch he may still pick up. I'm talking of some person who in his present situation may have held her own, may really have counted."

The "difference between them" is of course his ignorance of the positive role a sexual relation has played in Chad's development, and Strether, a little piqued by her pity, goes on to articulate his thought. He knows that Chad has an unfortunate *faible* for "mere wretches," but—James with mild irony has him "reasonably" explain—such a woman wouldn't account for the change in Chad. Although Strether's categories are gently mocked and his imagination is in error, he has still made an impressive stride. If he is confused as to the vehicle for Chad's improvement, it is because he now appreciates the scope and value of the improvement.

Later he will tell little Bilham:

"She keeps *him* up—she keeps the whole thing up . . . She's wonderful, wonderful, as Miss Barrace says; and he is, in his way, too; however, as a mere man, he may sometimes rebel and not feel that he finds his account in it. She has simply given him an immense moral lift, and what that can explain is prodigious. That's why I speak of it as a situation. It *is* one, if ever there was." And Strether, with his head back and his eyes on the ceiling, seemed to lose himself in the vision of it.

His companion attended deeply. "You state it much better than I could."

The mistake in Strether's "vision of it" is the same as in the earlier passage, but something remarkable has happened. Though Strether's imagination balks at the physical basis of Chad and

Madame de Vionnet's relationship, in his own way he now does full—even ideal—justice to their affair. Smugness and complacency have disappeared from his tone, and in their place is appreciative wonder. Having brooded at length upon their affair, Strether succeeds in expressing it as a formed, consistent, dramatic "situation." He has imagined it with a rightness that transcends his factual error, and little Bilham says no more than the truth.

Strether's mounting perception of the motives and behavior of those around him begins to bear fruit. Waymarsh, he makes out, will have cabled Mrs. Newsome about her ambassador's truancy. Maria wonders if this angers Strether, and he calmly replies, "Do I look in a great rage?" He goes on thoughtfully to piece together Waymarsh's rationale: "He has acted from the deepest conviction, with the best conscience and after wakeful nights." Maria, who may remember Strether's earlier indignant description of the "base, venal" woman, is struck by his tone of civilized lucidity and imaginative sympathy: "How wonderfully you take it! But you're always wonderful."

With his growing ability to penetrate appearances and to appreciate motives, Strether escapes the frightened insecurity, though not the discomfort, of his "double consciousness," and as the situation deteriorates he remains equal to its complications. When Waymarsh tells him Sarah is about to descend, he reflects: "Considering how many pieces had to fit themselves, it all fell, in Strether's brain, into a close rapid order. He saw on the spot what had happened, and what probably would yet; and it was all funny enough. It was perhaps just this freedom of appreciation that wound him up to his flare of high spirits. 'What is she coming *for?*—to kill me?' "

This intrepid urbanity, this daring to imagine and thus confront things he would earlier have avoided, has already warned Strether that Jim's silence in the taxi portends a general failure of perception on the part of the new ambassadors. Jim, furthermore, who is to convey unwittingly to Chad the ignominious fate of the Woollett businessman, "tells" Strether more in twenty minutes than he had in as many years: "He seemed to say that there was a whole side of life on which the perfectly usual *was* for leading Woollett business-men to be out of the question . . . Strether's imagination, as always, worked, and he asked himself if this side of life were not somehow connected, for those who figured on it, with the fact of marriage. Would *his* relation to it, had he married ten years before, have become now the same as Pocock's?" Inevitably approaching nearer and nearer to the main source of his uneasiness, Strether's expanding imagination closes with Mrs. Newsome herself; immovable and filled with her inadequate vision of things, *she* cannot be altered: " 'What it comes to [if one wants to change her]' said Strether, 'is that you've got morally and intellectually to get rid of her.' "

With his perception thus sharpened, Strether cannot help foreseeing that Chad will eventually leave it all to him: "I 'sort of' feel . . . that the whole thing will come upon me. Yes, I shall have every inch and every ounce of it. I shall be *used* for it—! . . . To the last drop of my blood." Consequently, Chad's reiterated declarations of faith sound ominously hollow to Strether's "imaginative mind." He sees that the young man will soon grow tired of Madame de Vionnet, and Chad's make-believe kick of the imaginary bribe further chills Strether with the impression of a "restless" boy doing "an irrelevant hornpipe or jig."

Virtually doomed to know all, Strether is helpless before his penetrating imagination. When Chad and Madame de Vionnet come floating down the river into his ken, he sees immediately and entirely what they are even before identifying who they are:

> For two very happy persons he found himself straightaway taking them—a young man in shirt-sleeves, a young woman easy and fair, who had pulled pleasantly up from some other place and, being acquainted with the neighbourhood, had known what this particular retreat could offer them. The air quite thickened, at their approach, with further intimations; the intimation that they were expert, familiar, frequent—that this wouldn't at all events be the first time. They knew how to do it, he vaguely felt.

The insistent impression of their familiarity with the neighborhood, with the inn, with themselves; the loosely sexual reference of "expert, familiar, frequent"; the heavily sexual implications of "this wouldn't at all events be the first time. They knew how to do it"— all these pitiless notations of Strether's unerring, educated imagination will remain lodged in his memory to point up, by contrast, the peculiar ignorance that also characterizes his imagination. The man who expertly takes in every detail of their intimacy, their annoyance, and their considering whether to "cut" him if he has not seen them is the same man who "almost blushed, in the dark, for the way he had dressed the possibility in vagueness, as a little girl might have dressed her doll. . . . He recognized at last that he had really been trying all along to suppose nothing."

To analyze Strether's experience apart from his imagination is to invite artificial distinctions. Strether's behavior and his vision are so intimately related—and both are so fully developed in this novel ("behavior" was conspicuously limited in *The Sacred Fount*)—that any final view of the novel is obliged to discuss them together. At this point, however, it seems worthwhile to attempt to isolate the curve of Strether's Parisian experience, its arc of deepening initiation and modified withdrawal.

Before joining Maria Gostrey in the garden at Chester, Strether reflects on the oddness of his position and on the sense of being launched in something new: "It had begun in fact already upstairs and before the dressing-glass . . . begun with a sharper survey of the elements of Appearance than he had for a long time been moved to make." His own physical appearance and that of others, the phenomena about him, begin to take on a mixed and intensifying interest. When he first enters Maria's Parisian apartment, his response is a characteristic compound of admiration expressed in biblical phrases that simultaneously imply mistrust: "wide as his glimpse had lately become of the empire of 'things,' what was before him still enlarged it; the lust of the eyes and the pride of life had indeed thus their temple." He becomes so initiated, however, into this source of pleasure that, when he later visits Madame de Vionnet's apartment, his appreciative faculties cause him to sense about her possessions "the air of supreme respectability, the consciousness . . . of private honour."

Nevertheless, Strether remains intermittently uncomfortable until he has an idea of what lies beneath the surfaces, what they conceal. Parisian conversation is vividly entertaining, but he wonders if it has, as in the metamorphosis of Waymarsh into Sitting Bull, any relation to truth: "You've all of you here so much visual sense that you've somehow all 'run' to it. There are moments when it strikes one that you haven't any other." When Miss Barrace whimsically agrees with his charge: "in the light of Paris one sees what things resemble . . . Everything, every one shows," Strether cannot resist asking, "But for what they really are?" to which she responds, "Oh I like your Boston 'really's'!" Charming people, delightful manners, playful conversations—she implies—convey their own meanings; and Strether must learn—like Maisie and the narrator of *The Sacred Fount*—to interpret such phenomena by their appearances alone rather than seek helplessly to discover the essences "really" within. And every now and then, as with the inscrutable Paris where "what seemed all surface one moment seemed all depth the next," he receives a slight jolt: "He made out in a moment that the youth was in earnest as he hadn't yet seen him; which in its turn threw a ray perhaps a trifle startling on what they had each up to that time been treating as earnestness."

Strether's growing appreciation of the physical world is also conveyed, as other critics have noted, by the mounting pleasure he takes in meals during his experience of Europe. Dining with Maria Gostrey by candlelight in London, Strether takes in "the rose-coloured shades and the small table and the soft fragrance of the lady—had anything to his mere sense ever been so soft?" Rising to the occasion, his "mere sense" proceeds to give way to the "uncontrolled perception that his friend's velvet band somehow added, in her appearance, to the value of every other item—to that of her smile and of the way she carried her head, to that of her complexion, of her lips, her teeth, her eyes, her hair." It is an observation and a catalogue Strether would have blushed to make earlier; desire and the appreciation of the human figure as something potentially lovely are awakening. "The lust of the eyes and the pride of life," moreover, are everywhere on display when he arrives in Paris. The aroma of sensuous nature groomed by art is wafted to Strether by the Parisian breeze: "the air had a taste as of something mixed with art, something that presented nature as a white-capped master-chef."

The epitome of the artful though simple perfection of the sensuous Parisian life is expressed—again in terms of a meal—through Strether's unforgettable luncheon with Madame de Vionnet at the restaurant on the quay:

> He was to feel many things on this occasion, and one of the
> first of them was that he had travelled far since that
> evening in London, before the theatre, when his dinner
> with Maria Gostrey . . . had struck him as requiring so
> many explanations. He had at that time gathered them in,
> the explanations . . . but it was at present as if he had either

soared above or sunk below them . . . he could somehow think of none that didn't seem to leave the appearance of collapse and cynicism easier for him than lucidity. How could he wish it to be lucid for others, for any one, that he, for the hour, saw reasons enough in the mere way the bright clean ordered waterside life came in at the open window?—the mere way Madame de Vionnet, opposite him over their intensely white table-linen, their *omelette aux tomates,* their bottle of straw-coloured Chablis, thanked him for everything almost with the smile of a child, while her grey eyes moved in and out of their talk, back to the quarter of the warm spring air, in which early summer had already begun to throb, and then back again to his face and their human questions.

The woman, the city, the food blend together and move him in a way that, he now feels, no explanation can account for. As overpoweringly real, attractive, self-justifying phenomena, they mean more than any abstraction in the form of a moral tag that can be leveled for or against them. It is only "the appearance of collapse and cynicism," a necessary step in the process of conversion that Strether—like little Bilham before him—undergoes, as his inadequate moral props fall beneath him and he begins to appreciate the sheer sensuous joy of sharing a simple—though elegant—meal, in a charming setting with an ardent woman. In so doing he shows how far he has come toward the "single boon" he desires, "the common unattainable art of taking things as they came."

Through being able to take Madame de Vionnet as she is, though this smashes his categories, he gains immeasurably in appreciation. When Sarah Pocock later lashes out at him, "Do you consider her even an apology for a decent woman?" he thinks to himself, "Ah there it was at last! . . . It was so much—so much; and she treated it, poor lady, as so little." The phrase "poor lady" turns out not to be wholly figurative; it is rigid and unappreciative Sarah Pocock, like Mrs. Touchett in *The Portrait of a Lady,* who is finally impoverished. The Cleopatra allusion for Madame de Vionnet is variously suggestive, as several critics have pointed out, but in no way more so than in indicating the impoverishment of not knowing Madame de Vionnet:

ANTONY: Would I had never seen her!
ENOBARBUS: O, sir, you had then left unseen a wonder
    ful piece of work; which not to have been blest
    withal would have discredited your travel.
                        (*Antony and Cleopatra*, 1.2.158–61)

Such a change in Strether has its source in his encountering and being altered by phenomena more inscrutable and lovely than any he has seen before. He returns from an early conversation with little Bilham and reports gaily to Waymarsh, "Well, I guess I don't know anything!" Learning that little Bilham has passed this bit of information on to Strether, Waymarsh is annoyed, but Strether considers it not as a reduction but as "somehow enlarging," something he has "found out from the young man." All of the toddling and rebirth metaphors associated with Strether point to his voluntary acceptance of a blank slate; Waymarsh, of course, never toddles. Thus prepared, Strether recognizes and richly appreciates Chad's transformation: "One wants, confound it, don't you see? . . . to enjoy anything so rare." "With such elements," he knows, "one can't count," can't analyze; just as, "thanks to one of the short-cuts of genius, she [Madame de Vionnet] had taken all his categories by surprise."

Shorn of his categories, Strether relies only on his individual faculty of appreciation, a faculty that depends upon context and cannot operate by remote control or across the sea. Mrs. Newsome cannot possibly appreciate Madame de Vionnet, because, as Strether has learned, "there's all the indescribable—what one gets only on the spot." When pressed by Sarah to account for himself, Strether's response is correspondingly uncategorical, not "lucid," but deeply appropriate:

I don't think there's anything I've done in any such calculated way as you describe. Everything has come as a sort of indistinguishable part of everything else. Your coming out belonged closely to my having come before you, and my having come was a result of our general state of mind. Our general state of mind had proceeded, on its side, from our queer ignorance, our queer misconceptions and confusions—from which, since then, an inexorable tide of light seems to have floated us into our perhaps still queerer knowledge.

What he has done is, devastatingly, to see for himself. "I couldn't, without my own impression, realise. She's a tremendously clever brilliant capable woman, and with an extraordinary charm on top of it all . . . I understand what a relation with such a woman—what such a high fine friendship—may be. It can't be vulgar or coarse, anyway—and that's the point."

Strether, of course, pays for such an impression, but not primarily because it is partly false nor because he will lose the security that otherwise awaits his return home. He pays most dearly, from beginning to end, because it is an impression, as he is well aware, that betrays a woman to whom he owes much and who has every reason, given her views and his commitment, to expect different behavior from him.

Nevertheless, confronting and accepting such a cost, Strether faces up to his new and "fatal perceptions" and begins to "let go." Since "he might perish by the sword as well as by famine," he decides to enjoy some of those things, including smoking with a lady, that he somehow never had occasion to do earlier. Little Bilham and Waymarsh both receive his impassioned counsel to live, and, having "missed the train" all his life, he catches, on the spur of the moment, a random one to the country. Wandering through the pastoral woods, he lounges luxuriantly about and freely chatters to himself in French, unhampered by the critical eye of others. Responding to artful appearances and the joys of sensuous living, forgetting his troublesome moral categories, nurturing his faculty of appreciation and finding that his desires themselves have been growing, Strether completes this stage of his initiation into European experience with a leisurely and elaborate celebration of his awakened appetite for life. He orders a sumptuous "repast" at the pastoral Cheval Blanc and, mentally savoring the feast to come, retires to the garden with his aperitif to enjoy the view of the river.

Before considering Strether's encounter with Chad and Madame de Vionnet, one further pattern of initiation must be traced: the transformation from spectator to performer. An elderly man half enviously, half complacently observing a world of strange, brilliant appearances is Strether's first conception of himself. He feels obliged to warn Maria Gostrey, "I come from Woollett Massachusetts." When she probes into the reason for this warning, he answers, "Why that you should find me too hopeless."

At the London theater with her as his guide, Strether is already becoming rejuvenated, but he is still awed by the performance at which he is a mere spectator. Characteristically he misjudges the melodrama he sees, regarding it as a work of art, just as later he will be aware of the artistic beauty of Chad's affair, initially regarded as a melodrama. The theater itself, Strether reflects, is a dubious source of entertainment for Mrs. Newsome's supposedly austere and authoritative ambassador: "He clearly hadn't come out in the name of propriety but to visit unattended equivocal performances." During another such "equivocal performance, Chad makes his fabulous stage entry, and Strether is clearly all agog, the fascinated spectator. At Gloriani's garden party and in Notre Dame, likewise, Strether plays the role of observer in the pageant of life unfolding itself.

A significant shift in sympathy, however, has taken place. Regretting the emptiness of his own youth, Strether now assents to what he sees and decides that, though he is to old for "the affair of life," he will do what he can for Madame de Vionnet, will "give her a sign. The sign would be that—though it was her own affair—he understood; the sign would be that—though it was her own affair— she was free to clutch. Since she took him for a firm object . . . he would do his best to *be* one." Caught between his intense desire to help and his multiple awareness that he is too old, that he is elsewhere committed, and that he knows both more and less than he ought to about "her own affair," Strether makes a cautious, in some ways unwilling and uninformed, but profound commitment to the new appearances. He steps into the act, and before long his nightmares are not of failing Mrs. Newsome but of failing Madame de Vionnet through a craven surrender to Sarah Pocock.

At the luncheon with Madame de Vionnet he takes from her an explanation of this new commitment more acute and concise than any he could proffer:

> "But for myself," she added, "the question is what *you* make."
>
> "Ah I make nothing. It's not my affair."
>
> "I beg your pardon. It's just there that, since you've taken it up and are committed to it, it most intensely becomes yours. You're not saving me, I take it, for your interest in myself, but for your interest in our friend. The one's at any rate wholly dependent on the other. You can't

in honour not see me through," she wound up, "because you can't in honour not see *him*."

Although she ignores or tactfully minimizes his interest in her as a motive, Madame de Vionnet unerringly points to the vision of Chad that Strether has, to the hilt, appreciated. Strether is "committed" indeed—he's up to his neck in the "affair"—because of the way, as her last words richly suggest, he has *seen* Chad. Imaginative vision thus fuses with Strether's active experience; seeing Chad leads "in honour" to seeing him through.

At Sarah's hotel room he recognizes instantly how compromised he is. Already convicted of being in Madame de Vionnet's boat, he has no options: "He took up an oar and, since he was to have the credit of pulling, pulled." Unmistakably active now, Strether shows how well he has assimilated the sophisticated and playful art of European manners. Madame de Vionnet, never more a *femme du monde* than now, engages in delightful, exaggerated love-play with Strether: "When does one ever see you? I wait at home and I languish. You'll have rendered me the service, Mrs. Pocock, at least . . . of giving me one of my much-too-rare glimpses of this gentleman."

Doubtless hearing for the first time the word "languish" used in connection with "Mr. Strether," Sarah, slightly unnerved, grants Madame de Vionnet her "natural due" and asserts that "the privilege of his society isn't a thing I shall quarrel about with any one." Gaily and intrepidly ignoring the unpleasant connotations of her remark, Strether leaps into the breach: "And yet, dear Sarah . . . I feel, when I hear you say that, that you don't quite do justice to the important truth of the extent to which—as you're also mine—I'm *your* natural due. I should like much better . . . to see you fight for me." A seasoned actor now, he accepts Madame de Vionnet's caressing attention and innuendo, reflecting that "it was indeed as if they were arranged, gathered for a performance, the performance of 'Europe' by his confederate and himself. Well the performance could only go on."

The performance does go on, and, instead of passively or blankly watching it, Strether is one of the stage managers, one of the few truly "in it" who perceive the hidden motive behind Chad's dazzling round of parties for his family. Miss Barrace, who habitually confuses Strether, joins with him now to "embroider the theme" of the delightful drama they're watching: "Oh I see the principle. If one didn't one would be lost. But when once one has got hold of it—." Their language, one notices, echoes the tutored Mrs. Briss of *The Sacred Fount* when she begins to "perceive," among the bewildering appearances before them, the hidden motives offered by the narrator: "When one knows it, it's all there. But what's that vulgar song?— 'You've got to know it first!' " "When one has had the 'tip' one looks back and sees things in a new light." No similarity points up contrasts more effectively than this one; the obsessive epistemological theme of *The Sacred Fount* is strictly subordinated to the larger concerns of the story in *The Ambassadors*: one has no doubt whatsoever that Strether and Miss Barrace *do* know. Earlier he would have been baffled, but Strether now not only understands the spectacle of European manners, he is credited, again by Miss Barrace, with being the indispensable performer of them all, the one on whom it all depends: "We know you as the hero of the drama, and we're gathered to see what you'll do."

Of course what complicates our response to Strether is our knowledge that if he is "the hero," he does not entirely understand the nature of "the drama" in which he participates. Appearances, after all, "must have a basis," and this basis Strether has consistently, almost willfully misunderstood. Europe is delightful, but at moments he sees through its charming facade: "Then there was something in the great world covertly tigerish, which came to him across the lawn and in the charming air as a waft from the jungle." Behind the dazzling manners of Gloriani's sophisticated garden party, he senses the interplay of veiled passions. Again, when Madame de Vionnet informs him of her calculated plan to "bring off" Jeanne's marriage, Strether inwardly winces: "Vaguely and confusedly he was troubled by it . . . He had allowed for depths, but these were greater . . . It was—through something ancient and cold in it—what he would have called the real thing."

One thinks of Osmond and Madame Merle attempting to "bring off" Pansy's marriage to Lord Warburton. But where that situation really was "hideous and unclean," Strether's uneasiness at the European convention of planned marriages seems to reflect as much on the incompleteness of his "Europeanized" state as on the brutality of the convention itself.

Strether determinedly throws off these moments of discomfiture. He prefers to view European appearances and traditions romantically, as emblems of Western civilization to be enjoyed and artistically embroidered by the appreciative imagination. Nowhere is such embroidering more in evidence than during his day of pastoral rambling. Here the various motifs of romance culminate.

Throughout the novel Strether has vicariously re-created his youth, and his trip to the country—in which he catches the train he had always missed—seems to actualize what had at first been metaphorical. Strether lives into the Lambinet painting he could not afford to buy years earlier: "it was all there, in short—it was what he wanted: it was Tremont Street, it was France, it was Lambinet. Moreover he was freely walking about in it." Not only does his youth seem to be recaptured and redeemed, but art and life come together; the rural scene "fell into a composition, full of felicity" such as only art or life perfected by form can offer. It all thus harmonizes with his vision of Chad as like a "pleasant perfect work of art," with his vision of Madame de Vionnet as a mythological goddess, and with his sense of the Parisian air as the perfecting instrument for lifting sensuous life into formal art.

He comfortably muses about the new role Madame de Vionnet now plays in his life, the pleasant danger of falling in love with her, the increasing intimacy between the two of them, with Chad "out of the picture." Strether himself remains all day in the picture, not once overstepping "the oblong gilt frame"; and he reflects on what was at bottom its spell: "that it was essentially more than anything else a scene and a stage, that the very air of the play was in the rustle of the willows and the tone of the sky." Having participated in "the performance of Europe," Strether feels familiar with the drama before him, and he enjoys deeply both the difference between this "picture" and Woollett and his own confidence in being able "to make one's account with what one lighted on."

Settling down for dinner at the Cheval Blanc, Strether reflects "that the picture and the play seemed supremely to melt together in the good woman's broad sketch of what she could do for her visitor's appetite." Appetite, picture, and play; youth and age; a sense of being initiated into European life and into the teasing possibility of love; the fusion of pastoral art and rural French life—all these come together before the moment of Strether's climactic meal, only to separate, a few minutes later, at the appearance of the real lovers. The romance has been true, he sees, in his mind alone: he is not a young lover, though he may muse about the possibility; he is not in

Madame de Vionnet's boat, though he may pull the oars as much as he wishes. The pastoral artistry emanates as much from himself as from the scene; the real drama—not the imagined picture—is one, finally, for which "he knew he had been, at bottom, neither prepared nor proof."

The meal the three eat together is but a shadow of that sumptuous feast he had confidently ordered a few minutes earlier; his "appetite," so to speak, has received a deathblow. "There had been simply a *lie* in the charming affair—a lie on which one could now, detached and deliberate, perfectly put one's finger. It was with the lie that they had eaten and drunk and talked and laughed." He sees now, as Madame de Vionnet weaves a story out of thin air, the artifice involved in their art and in his artistic, embroidering imagination: "What it all came to had been that fiction and fable *were,* inevitably, in the air, and not as a simple term of comparison, but as a result of things said."

Yet the decorous lie is still preferable to any vulgar rending of veils: "He had had in the actual case to make-believe more than he liked, but this was nothing, it struck him, to what the other event would have required. Could he, literally, quite have faced the other event?" Increasingly, thankful for the grace of her behavior under stress, Strether comes to realize "that their eminent 'lie,' Chad's and hers, was simply after all such an inevitable tribute to good taste as he couldn't have wished them not to render . . . he could trust her to make deception right. As she presented things the ugliness—goodness knew why—went out of them." Strether's present attitude toward the Parisian world of intriguing appearances is a precarious balance of trust and disenchantment. The difficulty of maintaining such a balance is increased, moreover, by his gradual discovery of the liabilities of his imagination and of the cost of the kind of living he had earlier exhorted like Bilham to attain.

The exemplar of ideal "living" has, of course, been Chad, and Strether's developing attitude toward him greatly influences the shape of Strether's own behavior. The elder man's first impression was of a transcendent, miraculous change. Chad has become a smooth and polished man of the world, one "to whom things had happened and were variously known." He has been artistically formed, "put into a firm mould and turned successfully out." Strether immediately correlates this with his vision of Chad as "the young man marked out by women; and for a concentrated minute the dignity, the comparative austerity . . . of this character affected him almost with awe. . . . Yes, experience was what Chad did play on him."

Chad has lived, Strether intuits, in those undefined and exciting ways *he* never knew, and they remain undefined for several reasons. Strether can only guess at Chad's achievement, since it corresponds to a vague yearning rather than a precise knowledge. Encounters with women; a casual self-possession; expressive, graceful, assured manners; doing easily what one likes; being the center of relations in which the other parties are pleased to play "subsidiary" roles; enjoying and being "expert familiar" with the spectacle of life; above all knowing "how to do it"—these are hazily inferred by Strether as components of Chad's awesome experience. But there are reasons beyond Strether's inevitable vagueness for the novel's refusal to substantiate in greater detail Chad's achievement; this achievement is seriously called into question as the novel progresses; James never intended the reader to respond to it as entirely solid.

Beyond this, I would suggest, lies James's refusal ever to create a convincing image of experience composed in the terms of Chad's presumed achievement. Strether may yearn for those achievements, may passionately urge little Bilham not to miss them, but James never, as a novelist, makes them credible. They are rendered hazily because they are not a viable value in the Jamesian world. The Chad Newsomes in his fiction are not shown attaining their experience, and the internal logic within James's novels succeeds ultimately in casting doubt on the very goals of such characters. It is as though twenty-five years earlier James faced the novelistic (and perhaps personal) choice of pursuing the kind of experience available to Roderick or the kind available to Rowland. As I suggested earlier, the Roderick figure does reappear in James's fiction, but it is to those toward whom he is tender—Newman at the very end, Isabel, Ralph Touchett, Hyacinth, Maisie, Milly, but not Chad—that James grants the superior imagination and disillusionment, the distinctive, perhaps compulsive experience of a life filled with perception and deprived of all else that he first embodied in Rowland Mallet. Strether, one finally sees, can no more attain, or ultimately endorse, Chad's experience than Rowland can Roderick's.

To live as Chad lives, in the rich possession of passion and intimacy, is, throughout James's fiction, to create costs and impose burdens that, once imaginatively realized, James's distinctive heroes can never permit themselves. If one is to live like Chad, one cannot imagine and respond like Strether; if one is to appreciate with Strether's full intensity, one must forego the shared intimacy and experience of Chad's way of life. It is the salient feature of James's moral world that physical experience and activity are presented (and in some cases distorted) in such a way as to be inaccessible to his imaginative heroes and heroines. Strether will learn about Chad what Isabel Archer finally perceives about herself: "to take a deep, self-developing breath is, morally speaking, to cause those nearby almost to suffocate."

Chad's "acquired high polish" involves a considerable amount of "hardness," and Strether increasingly realizes the difficulty of moving the young man into alignment with Strether's vision of him. Chad is his own man, handles things his own way, listens to Strether without responding to him. Such inscrutable, self-absorbed, inflexible self-possession leads Strether anew to realize "the truth that everything came happily back with him to his knowing how to live . . . He [Strether] didn't want, luckily, to prevent Chad from living, but he was quite aware that even if he had he would himself have thoroughly gone to pieces. It was in truth essentially by bringing down his personal life to a function all subsidiary to the young man's own that he held together."

The tone of the passage is slightly ambiguous toward Chad's unique gift. "Living," as the younger man exemplifies it, increasingly resembles exploiting, and Strether's perception of Chad's behavior at the Cheval Blanc completes the revolution of his own point of view: "It was a part of the deep impression for Strether . . . that Chad in particular could let her know he left it to her. He habitually left things to others, as Strether was so well aware, and it in fact came over our friend in these meditations that there had been as yet no such vivid illustration of his famous knowing how to live."

As his vision of Chad darkens, so, in a more complicated way, does his idealized version of Madame de Vionnet. When, flushed, she breaks into French at the Cheval Blanc, he sees her as, after all, a Frenchwoman speaking her language as millions of others do. At the same time he appreciates her rare talent for making "deception right," the "tribute to good taste" that her charming fictions express. But it is at Madame de Vionnet's apartment, for the last time, that his vision of her clarifies itself. Desperate over her coming loss she clings to and even—a little—pretends a romantic interest in Strether to keep him by her in Paris.

It is a difficult scene to interpret, and Madame de Vionnet may not be pretending at all. Her words to Strether are impassioned and sound sincere, but it is hard not to accept Strether's view that Chad is at the center of her feelings and he, Strether, is appealed to as a temporary refuse and pawn. Still, Strether's reinforced detachment and his sexual timidity probably blind him to the degree of candor actually behind her outburst; he has lavished upon her an appreciative admiration that no one else, not even Chad, has shown, and it causes her genuine anguish to lose, as she thinks, his respect. The mixture in her of sex and affection, of art and innocence has always baffled Strether, and probably never more than now. He is more perturbed by this apparent duplicity than by what he had discovered in the country, and he intuitively senses the source of her trouble:

> What was at bottom the matter with her, embroider as she might and disclaim as she might . . . was simply Chad himself. It was of Chad she was after all renewedly afraid; the strange strength of her passion was the very strength of her fear; she clung to *him,* Lambert Strether, as to a source of safety she had tested, and, generous graceful truthful as she might try to be, exquisite as she was, she dreaded the term of his being within reach. With this sharpest perception yet, it was like a chill in the air to him, it was almost appalling, that a creature so fine could be, by mysterious forces, a creature so exploited.

What brings her down, what keeps her from being quite as "generous graceful truthful" as he had once imagined is just that "strange strength of her passion" which he now discerns beneath her charm, analogous to that earlier glimpse of passion lurking beneath the splendid pageant of manners in Gloriani's garden. It chills and almost appalls him that even she is compromised "by mysterious forces" beyond her control, "exploited" by the current of her feelings for Chad, a victim—and to that degree vulgar—of her own desires. Exploited by her own passion, she will, he thinks, in the most well-intended but also desperate way, exploit him as a means of solacing herself or keeping Chad by her. He sees for the first time and tells her that she's afraid for her life.

At this she breaks down, and as he witnesses her torment he almost ceases to think of her personally at all—

> as if he could think of nothing but the passion, mature, abysmal, pitiful, she represented, and the possibilities she betrayed. She was older for him tonight, visibly less exempt from the touch of time; but she was as much as ever the finest and subtlest creature, the happiest apparition, it had been given him, in all his years, to meet; and yet he could see her there as vulgarly troubled, in very truth, as a maidservant crying for her young man. The only thing was she judged herself as the maidservant wouldn't; the weakness of which wisdom, the dishonour of which judgment, seemed but to sink her lower.

Like the narrator of *The Scared Fount* reflecting on May Server, Strether—sympathetic but quite detached and resolutely passive now—sees Madame de Vionnet less as a person than a "wasted and dishonoured symbol" of "the possibilities of our common nature." When he does see her as a person, it is to note her bondage to time and passion, to her physical condition as a human being. While the ethereal emblem of French civilization is timeless, the flesh and blood woman he sees before him is "vulgarly" distraught, like "a maidservant crying for her young man." Worse, she is unfortunate enough to judge herself by a "higher" standard, without being able to alter the course on which her passions have led her, and this "seemed but to sink her lower." What he most recoils from, however, what he considers "the real coercion" is "to see a man ineffably adored." Just as "a man" has no business, in the light of Strether's sensibilities, being "ineffably adored," so, in equally generic terms, does the revelation of intimacy disturb him: "intimacy, at such a point, was *like* that—and what in the world else would one have wished it to be like?"

The whole business of physical human intimacy goes obscurely against his loftier conceptions of human behavior; what he had indeed expected, as she so painfully sensed, was that she would be "well, sublime!" With its connotation of ethereality, "sublime" is the appropriate word for Strether's vision of human beings who have, he imagines, risen beyond their physical desires. It is part of that ideal pastoral fusion of nature and art that came to an end at the Cheval Blanc, a fusion that Strether, like Isabel, must believe in before he can so ardently expound the gospel of "living." With the downfall of his palace of thought, he retreats, slightly but significantly, into the role in which he will remain—the sympathetic but detached observer. Experience has been wonderful but never quite so grand as that vision of it created by his imagination, and, when Madame de Vionnet declares, "I've wanted you too," he answers truthfully, "Ah but you've *had* me!" For imaginative intimacy is the only plane on which he can consent to be "had"; from any other form of intimacy—with Madame de Vionnet and later with Maria Gostrey—he gently but firmly withdraws.

Playfully accepting Strether's "daring" invitation to luncheon on the quay, Madame de Vionnet had remarked that "her affairs would go to smash, but hadn't one a right to one's snatch of scandal when one was prepared to pay?" A great deal of Strether's experience is concerned with perceiving the ugliness of unpaid debts and the expense of paid ones. The most damning aspect of Mrs. Newsome's and the Pococks' blindness is that they want the finished product safe at home again, without paying the artist for her labors. "The business [of effecting Chad's transformation] hadn't been easy; it had taken time and trouble, it had cost, above all, a price." The price— Chad's relationship with Madame de Vionnet—is what they refuse to consider; moreover, Chad gives signs of ignoring it himself. Strether reminds him that "more has been done for you, I think, than I've ever seen done . . . by one human being for another." Sure of failure at the end, he helplessly upbraids Chad, "You'll be a brute, you know—you'll be guilty of the last infamy—if you ever forsake her."

But Strether himself is in a similar predicament; quite like Chad, he is reminded by Maria Gostrey: "Well, you owe more to women than any man I ever saw." The main debt he permits himself to recognize, however, is the one to Mrs. Newsome, and the honoring of it effectively shapes his last words to Maria Gostrey: "That, you see, is my only logic. Not, out of the whole affair, to have got anything for myself." He came to Europe, his conscience insists, not for himself but as Mrs. Newsome's ambassador; he can never accept what Europe has given him for himself unless he comes home, in a sense, still as her ambassador. The "miracle" that he too has undergone would become "monstrous," like Chad's, if it were entirely at her expense. If this prevents his "living," it is because, as he becomes more and more convinced, living implies putting the burden on others' shoulders, not paying one's deepest debts.

Chad is not so transformed after all, Strether comes finally to see: "She had made him better, she had made him best, she had made him anything one would; but it came to our friend with supreme queerness that he was none the less only Chad. . . . The work, however admirable, was . . . of the strict human order." It then strikes him as "marvelous" that such a one "should be so transcendently prized."

Strether, too, is finally less transformed than the reader has romantically imagined. His youth has, in a certain sense, been taken from him again; he has all along been slightly more of a confused spectator and less of an initiated actor than he had imagined; and he has found himself in a Woollett-like way shocked, "neither prepared nor proof" for his discovery at the Cheval Blanc. The exciting feeling of shared knowledge with Maria Gostrey and the Parisian sophisticates has hidden the fact that, in his innocent delusion, he has always been alone. He wonders now how he can face Maria Gostrey's "What on earth . . . had you then supposed?" But he does face it; he resists "a revulsion in favour of the principles of Woollett," and in a narrower sense he has indeed been transformed. The idols of his heyday, however—youth, appetite, the illusion of freedom, in a word, living—have been seriously challenged.

Youth now awakens in Strether feelings of apprehension as much as of yearning. That Chad is younger than Madame de Vionnet becomes an ominous fact, and even more ominous are Chad's youthful protestations: " 'I give you my word of honour,' he frankly rang out, 'that I'm not a bit tired of her.' Strether at this only gave him a stare; the way youth could express itself was again and again a wonder . . . he spoke of being 'tired' of her almost as he might have spoken of being tired of roast mutton for dinner." Later, with some awe, Strether tells Maria, "He asks how one can dream of his being tired. But he has all life before him." Here Chad's marvelous youth has been transformed into a vast arena for future infidelities and "affairs"; Strether stares at what "living" may yet mean for the young man.

Appetite is an ambiguous motif in the novel, since Strether's enjoyment of it has been gentle and restricted. At the Cheval Blanc his cultivation of it reaches its peak and subsides thereafter into an acceptance or understanding of others' desires. Certainly insofar as it has reference to sexual intimacy, Strether's appetite has always appeared to be moderate, and his diffidence in these matters gives point to the grotesque comedy of Jim's description of Mrs. Newsome and Sarah as voracious beasts, and of Mrs. Newsome sitting up "All night, my boy—for *you!*" The figure of being devoured is related to the hint of something "covertly tigerish" in Gloriani's world and to the marks of passion that deface Madame de Vionnet's beauty. Human passion threatens his need to be inviolate, implies an intimacy he is unwilling and unable to accept, be it from either Madame de Vionnet or Maria Gostrey.

If the illusion of freedom has any positive meaning for Strether at the end, it is surely no longer based on the vision of Chad's transformation, as his exhortation to little Bilham had been. Unrestricted self-development flourishes only at the expense of Madame de Vionnet's continuous sacrifice. The sacred fount metaphor of abysmal exploitation-sacrifice is relevant here, for it indicates how James, in his depiction of even the loveliest human intimacy, expresses primarily a dubious development and a real diminishment. Chad feels restless, wants to "live" a little more. He will neglect his unpayable debt; as little Bilham saw at the beginning, he cannot be free and good at the same time.

What it comes to is that Strether has had a vision of sublime relationships, a vision that the actual conditions can never meet. Maria tells Strether that "it would be difficult to see now quite what degree of ceremony [on the part of Chad and Madame de Vionnet] properly meets your case." Strether concedes, "Of course, my attitude toward them is extraordinary," to which she returns, "Just so; so that one may ask one's self what style of proceeding on their part can altogether match it. The attitude of their own that won't pale in its light they've doubtless still to work out." The "sublime" generosity of his imagination is, inevitably, what keeps him immaculate, isolated, doomed to disillusionment. He vanishes, in Quentin Anderson's acute phrase, into "the limbo of a lonely righteousness." No "style of proceeding" can match his vision of behavior; Madame de Vionnet weeps because, merely flesh and blood, she cannot be "sublime." Intimacy and passion, as James sees them with their full complement of exploitation, self-surrender, anguish, and even mutilation, are to be approached through the prism of the idealizing and enriching imagination, rather than through personal experience.

Strether's unpaid debt to Maria Gostrey is the result partly of having "seen for himself" that "intimacy . . . was *like* that" and partly of "clinging again intensely to the strength of his position, which was precisely that there was nothing in it for himself." It is, however, a position ultimately untenable, for if Strether is right in seeing that the betrayal of Mrs. Newsome's embassy is warranted only through disinterest, he remains unjustified in entering Maria Gostrey's life, profiting greatly from her, and then discarding her when he has had his fill: "the time seemed already far off when he had held out his small thirsty cup to the spout of her pail. Her pail was scarce touched now, and other fountains had flowed for him; she fell into her place as but one of his tributaries." This is the same prose James used to describe the sacred fount relationship—"we had suddenly caught Long in the act of presenting his receptacle at the sacred fount"—and it indicates the way in which Strether exploits Maria Gostrey. Ignoring his debt to her with an apparently unruffled conscience, he leaves her, in Laurence Holland's words, "in the affair of art, the affair of memory and imagination, rather than in the affair of life which she hopes for."

The return to solitary spectatorship is not, after all, surprising. Strether's deepest experiences have all along been his inner vibrations to a world of marvelous appearances: "the fact was that his perception of the young man's identity . . . had been quite one of the sensations that count in life." Even when alone, like Spencer Brydon in "The Jolly Corner," Strether can spend, while waiting for Chad, "an hour full of strange suggestions, persuasions, recognitions; one of those that he was to recall, at the end of his adventure, as the particular handful that most had counted." "It was nothing new to him . . . that a man might have—at all events such a man as he—an amount of experience out of any proportion to his adventures."

Strether lives most intensely at the level of inner response, of appreciation; and the course of the novel is to demonstrate how beautifully he rises to the spectacle of European culture: "Call it then life . . . call it poor dear old life simply that springs the surprise. Nothing alters the fact that the surprise is paralysing, or at any rate engrossing—all, practically, hang it, that one sees, that one *can* see." Seeing, reverberating internally to the spectacle—these are the essence of Strether's experience, and they imply for him a paralysis of sorts; if one is to see with full wondrous appreciation, one can't very well do anything else.

Some such paralysis is implied, I think, by Strether's absorbed rehearsal and mental reenactment of great moments that recur throughout the novel. The fusion (discussed earlier) of past and future tenses that James uses so often to describe Strether's responses serves to release an experience from its immediate bondage to space and time and to allow it to reverberate internally and as long as Strether desires to appreciate it. Strether then possesses his experience forever, but he is equally possessed by it, able to render it, as time goes on, more and more ideal justice, but consequently unable, while cherishing the wonder of his augmenting past, to live in other ways during the present.

Little Bilham seems to embody a similar stance toward experience, and he sheds an interesting light on Strether's earlier outburst in Gloriani's garden: "Didn't you adjure me, in accents I shall never forget, to see, while I've a chance, everything I can?—and *really* to see, for it must have been that only you meant." Strether, however, had not urged little Bilham "to see," but rather "to live"; one surely felt at that point in the novel that something more was meant than perception ("—and now I'm old," Strether had recognized, "too old at any rate for what I see"). Not "seeing" but "what" he saw was the object of Strether's yearning—the sensuous fulfillment so absent from his own youth.

Later, as the novel begins in its various ways to call this vision into question, an essential shift occurs: the imagined life is gradually replaced by the life of imagination. Strether develops his generous and appreciative vision beyond the point where life can actually meet it, and he abandons life, if it comes to that, rather than his imaginative commitment to that vision. That his vision exceeds the facts is, after all, no reason to discard it, for it has served him well. He has had his youth in the same way that he has had Madame de Vionnet: vicariously, imaginatively, ideally.

Moved by a new vision of life's possibilities, Strether has acted for others in behalf of their youth. His tribute began as vicarious, but gingerly he commenced a new life of his own, with new relations, a new outlook. Inevitably his imagination, embroidering the theme, exceeded reality, and he ends by taking a quiet step in retreat to what is his only acceptable physical role: a slightly chastened but mellow middle-aged observer. His youth, which took place in his imagination, is now over; he has, as it were, "grown up" to himself and regained the age at which he entered the novel. But now, unlike then, he has the right to his fifty-five years, for the blank decades between childhood and middle age have been miraculously redeemed in the past six months. It is not that he has grown older but that he has, finally, matured. He now can confront what they all along have suspected back home—a liaison between Chad Newsome and some French woman—but he confronts it with a perceptive generosity undreamed of in Woollett. And he can do this because the real, "all comically, all tragically," has been combined and confused with a romantic vision of supremely civilized human relationships. If Strether's understanding of the combination accounts for his charity, so his understanding of the confusion explains his final, chosen withdrawal.

In the service of that vision he has had his youth, and it is one that can be caressingly perpetuated through memory and imagination, just as it was founded on these faculties. If it is empty of all else, including the shared intimacy and passion of a human relationship, it is because Strether has never, in either of his youths, deeply sought or experienced these things, but rather the vision of them, at first despaired of and now attained. That this is accepted by Strether with wit and poise, that it is enough for him, makes him the most charming imaginative hero in what seems to me James's most perfect work of art and, at the same time, the hero who indicates most clearly the narrow beauty of his creator's vision of life.

The Articulation of Time in *The Ambassadors*

Albert A. Dunn

"This eternal time-question is accordingly, for the novelist, always there and always formidable," James avers in the preface to *Roderick Hudson*. To maintain verisimilitude and to adhere to the laws of literary composition, the novelist, he continues, must find some means of giving the impression of the passage of time. Doing so enables him to portray not only the significance of his tale, but also the substance and surface of it. James proposes that the novelist can give the effect of time's passage by observing time as it operates upon a central consciousness. The novelist won't, then, show events except as they are registered upon that consciousness. In this way he meets the requirements of both verisimilitude and narrative organization; he can foreshorten his composition without similarly foreshortening his realistic time scheme.

The preface to *The Ambassadors* points to an even further refinement of this answer to the time-question. Though rejoicing in the quality of the mind which he was to render, James decided to deny Strether the free rein of first-person narration. Enforcing upon his hero the necessity of attending to the stiffer proprieties of his social role, James forbids Strether the "terrible *fluidity* of self-revelation" that a first-person account would entail. Instead the novelist controls what we see of the activities of Strether's consciousness by ordering the narrative according to a scheme that is determined in part by calendar, clock, or what we shall call social

From *Criticism* 14, no. 2 (Spring 1972). © 1972 by Wayne State University Press.

time. Strether, like his creator, must attend to surfaces. In fact, it is through Strether's consciousness that James renders those surfaces so adroitly. But surfaces are outside of consciousness in the social world through which Strether must move. In other words, if Strether is shown through what Ian Watt calls a mental continuum, his mental activities are nevertheless related to the social continuum. Social time is noted throughout the novel. It helps to structure the social world to which Strether must respond.

We experience social time through both Strether's apprehension of it and the narrator's specification of it. At the opening of most chapters—usually in the first sentence—the time is somehow indicated: Waymarsh is not to arrive till evening; Strether and Waymarsh spend that evening talking together; on the following morning Maria Gostrey has already breakfasted when Strether enters the coffee-room; Strether goes to the theatre with Maria on his third evening in London; next we are with him on his second morning in Paris. Generally, this notation is continued throughout the novel; the only obvious exceptions occur in book 5, which is devoted almost entirely to "the Sunday of the next week" spent in Gloriani's garden. Even then—when in the middle of the third chapter the narrative moves to the next day—the time is noted.

Social time is underscored because Strether's mission involves a problem of social knowledge. He must penetrate to the truth of a situation that is presented to him in entirely social terms. "You can't make out over here what people do know," he tells Waymarsh. Yet that is in fact part of his task—to discover what others do know. That so much of Strether's mental activity is devoted to reflection on the past and speculation on the future indicates the great extent to which social surfaces and social time absorb his energies.

And certainly, too, those energies that are devoted to his attempt "to gain time" are expansive. The result of his appreciation of social beauty, they permit him not only to recognize the latent possibility of another self, but in large measure to realize that self as well.

I. TIME AND KNOWING

If then we experience in the novel a density of temporal relationships, its source is located largely in Strether's response to social time. Hisayoshi Watanabe has pointed out that Strether's reaction to social experience is often retrospective. The recording of his perceptions, in other words, lags somewhat behind the actual events, while our focus is upon the working of Strether's mind rather than the actions it reflects.

Aside from the use of the past perfect tense, other methods contribute to our sense that Strether's is a retrospective mode of apprehension. James several times jumps the narrative forward to examine Strether's later reactions to the scene at hand. Twice during his first visit to Madame de Vionnet, Strether is shown through this technique. "He was amazed afterwards to think how simply and quietly he had met it," we are told of his response to Madame de Vionnet's question about his relationship with Mrs. Newsome. And shortly, following Strether's compliment to Jeanne, the narrator interposes Strether's later reaction: "The mother's eagerness with which Madame de Vionnet jumped at this was to come back to him later as beautiful in its grace."

The effect of this technique is to give added depth to Strether's response to the present scene. Depending upon the retrospective bent of Strether's mind, the device is also part of the novel's technical apparatus, which continually and unobtrusively moves backward and forward along the continuum of social time to present Strether's consciousness from various temporal perspectives.

Time is also used in this way to indicate Strether's befuddlement. In relation to the more or less immediate moment in social time, Strether's dilemma is often seen from a future perspective. Chad takes Strether to meet Madame de Vionnet for the first time:

> He afterwards scarce knew, absurd as it may seem, what had then quickly occurred. The moment concerned him, he felt, more deeply than he could have explained, and he had a subsequent passage of speculation as to whether, on walking off with Chad, he hadn't looked either pale or red.

This later reaction is then compared to his present sensations:

> The only thing he was clear about was that, luckily, nothing indiscreet had in fact been said, and that Chad himself was more than ever . . . wonderful.

If the past is always part of the present—"always spreading out like a drop of oil on consciousness," as Georges Poulet asserts—then future befuddlement is a means of indicating the quality of present experience. Strether is greatly disconcerted by the immediate prospect of his meeting Madame de Vionnet, and having few perceptions to feed upon, he is unable to arrive at a significant estimation of what he has experienced.

Most often Strether's temporal consciousness works by reinterpreting the past in light of the present. This is, of course, the major action of the book: Strether reinterprets past perspectives in view of present perceptions. But it is also an aspect of the more local workings of his mind. Taking another passage from book five, we can observe him as he revalues his impression of Madame de Vionnet after meeting her daughter:

> She stood there quite pink, a little frightened, prettier and prettier and not a bit like her mother. There was in this last particular no resemblance but that of youth to youth; and here was in fact suddenly Strether's sharpest impression. It went wondering, dazed, embarrassed, back to the woman he had just been talking with; it was revelation in the light of which he already saw she would become more interesting. So slim and fresh and fair, she had yet put forth this perfection; so that for really believing it of her, for seeing her to any such developed degree as a mother, comparison would be urgent. Well, what was it now but fairly thrust upon him?

Strether's most important impression of Madame de Vionnet is not presented through their immediate social encounter, but rather results from his retrospective estimation of her in the presence of her daughter. That impression must, furthermore, be based upon his rather scant initial response to the mother. He builds upon past impressions. When those impressions are inadequate or inaccurate, his subsequent reactions and assessments are necessarily either limited or inaccurate. This assumes, of course, that he would have no future contact with the person whom he is trying to judge. Subsequent encounters form the material for other retrospections and, therefore, other judgments.

James indicates this turn of mind in his hero through several narrative intrusions. One is particularly overt. After telling us what Strether was to remember about his countryside encounter with Chad and Madame de Vionnet, James inserts:

> When he reached home that night, however, he knew he
> had been, at bottom, neither prepared nor proof; and since
> we have spoken of what he was, after his return, to recall
> and interpret, it may as well immediately be said that his
> real experience of these few hours put on, in that belated
> vision—for he scarce went to bed till morning—the aspect
> that is most to our purpose.

The real experience is most fully interpreted later. Again, the
interpretation of that experience is what the narrative—having given
us the surfaces—can now explore.

But James does not stop at this. Having cast the whole scene
into this framework, he proceeds to explore simultaneously the
social reality and the interpretation it engenders. James makes it clear
that the interpretation merely makes wholly conscious what had
been present to Strether at the time:

> He then knew more or less how he had been affected—he
> but half knew at the time. There had been plenty to affect
> him even after, as has been said, they had shaken down; for
> his consciousness, though muffled, had its sharpest mo-
> ments during this passage, a marked drop into innocent
> friendly Bohemia.

The present moment, as experienced even through a muffled consciousness, provides the material for judgment. But judgment does
not operate fully until the present has receded and the assault of
images has abated. Strether must, in other words, become conscious
of what he already half-knows before he is able to pass judgment
upon it. That his consciousness is thus dependent upon time permits
him to give and withhold value through the agency of his memory;
later I will show how memory acts as an indication of the values that
Strether comes to adopt.

Strether is aware of his mind's propensities, and uses them to
control his social behavior. In the first chapter he is shown groping
in his overcoat just to gain time, to prepare himself, that is, for his
walk around Chester with Maria Gostrey. Late in the novel, after
receiving a note from Madame de Vionnet, he goes to the telegraph
office "with a directness that almost confessed to a fear of the danger
of delay. He might have been thinking that if he didn't go before he
could think he wouldn't perhaps go at all." This later self-awareness

indicates the great extent to which Strether has become cognizant of his own processes. It is through time that he grows to that awareness. Generally speaking, time is used to demonstrate Strether's particular quality of mind; specifically, it serves as a counter to measure both the accuracy of his perceptions of the social world and the extent of his self-awareness.

II. Time and Space

Strether is also aware of how readily accessible the past is to him. He calls upon it to provide a means of understanding his new experience in Europe. The comparisons with his personal past are innumerable, but probably most striking among them are those concerned with his first trip abroad—particularly those surrrounding the lemon-colored volumes. The books that he sees in the Paris shops, and that he won't buy until he has made contact with Chad, remind him of the books that he had bought on his first trip to Europe. They recall to him the "invocation of the finer taste" which his earlier purchase bespoke, and make him ask: "What had become of the sharp initiation they represented?" Later, in the presence of Madame de Vionnet's pink and green leather-bound volumes, Strether again recalls the paper-bound books he had wished to purchase. This time the green-covered revue is also mentioned, adding yet another dimension to the temporal structure:

> There were books, two or three, on a small table near his chair, but they hadn't the lemon-coloured covers with which his eye had begun to dally from the hour of his arrival and to the opportunity of a further acquaintance with which he had a fortnight now altogether succumbed. On another table, across the room, he made out the great *Revue;* but even that familiar face, conspicuous in Mrs. Newsome's parlours, scarce counted here as a modern one. He was sure on the spot—and afterwards knew he was right—that this was a touch of Chad's own hand.

To the extent that consciousness destroys the division between past and present, we might consider it spatial. In *The Ambassadors,* however, what Joseph Frank defines as spatial form seems only minimally present, for Strether continually distinguishes and labels past and present. He is too time-conscious to permit the past and present to be confused or blended. When spatial unity is seemingly attempted, when, for instance, he sees Chad on the balcony in the same position in which he had first seen little Bilham, it seems to emphasize not the distortion of time but its passage—and with its passage, Strether's education. This does not mean that James is unaware of the potentialities of spatial form, but that he uses spatiality in *The Ambassadors* in a different, more limited way: spatiality is used to portray Strether's desire for a momentary respite from the complexities of time.

In Notre Dame Strether attempts in his desire for simplicity to reduce the historical past "to the convenient terms of Victor Hugo." He had come there originally to find "a refuge from the obsession of his problem," acknowledging to himself that this refuge could be "only for the moment." When attempting "to reconstitute a past" in Hugo's simple terms, he is involved in a spatially represented exploration of the cathedral. "He was aware," we are told, "of having no errand in such a place but the desire not to be, for the hour, in certain other places." His escape is admittedly momentary; the contrast between the outside world and the cathedral does not entail stopped time. But the problems of the outside are absent from the cathedral: "Justice was outside, in the hard light, and injustice too; but one was as absent as the other from the air of the long aisles and the brightness of the many altars." And when Strether contemplates the woman who turns out to be Madame de Vionnet, all of the description is of angles and planes. The woman is "not in any degree bowed," but "strangely fixed," while Strether notices that "she had placed herself, as he never did, within focus of the shrine" and that "her back, as she sat, was turned to him." Even Strether's relation to the woman and to the cathedral itself, that is to say, is spatially represented. Though certainly part of this episode's meaning resides in Strether's lack of initiations and in the irony of his meeting Madame de Vionnet when attempting to escape his problem, the fact that the escape from time is spatially represented indicates some use of spatial metaphor.

This desire to escape perplexities is again represented in spatial terms late in the novel. Waiting for Chad's return, Strether indulges a bemused death-longing:

> It amused him to say to himself that he might for all the
> world have been going to die—die resignedly; the scene

was filled for him with so deep a death-bed hush, so
melancholy a charm. That meant the postponement of
everything else—which made so for the quiet lapse of life;
and the postponement in especial of the reckoning to
come—unless indeed the reckoning to come were to be
one and the same thing with extinction. It faced him, the
reckoning, over the shoulder of much interposing experience—which also faced him; and one would float to it
doubtless duly through these caverns of Kubla Khan.

Strether's sense of timeless drifting is portrayed, it seems to me, in
the image of the spatial relationship between himself and his
experience, and in the reference to the caverns of Kubla Khan. The
spatial elements emphasize the influence of both past and future on
the present. Part of James's technique for portraying Strether's
consciousness, these spatial elements distort the time scheme to
depict Strether's present state of mind in terms of past and future.
But as technique they should be distinguished from memory, which
is one of the consolations provided Strether and, too, a thematic
consideration.

Spatiality is used far more extensively in the novel. At times
spatial comparisons are coupled with temporal ones. When Strether
takes Madame de Vionnet to the cafe on the quay, the scene is
presented in terms of temporal and spatial elements:

It was on this pleasant basis of costly disorder, consequently, that they eventually seated themselves, on either
side of a small table, at a window adjusted to the busy quay
and the shining barge-burdened Seine; where, for an hour,
in the matter of letting himself go, of diving deep, Strether
was to feel that he had touched bottom. He was to feel
many things on this occasion, and one of the first of them
was that he had travelled far since that evening in London,
before the theatre. . . . He had at that time gathered them
in, the explanations—he had stored them up; but it was at
present as if he had either soared above or sunk below
them—he couldn't tell which.

First, the stage is set in terms of both space and time: the small table,
the window, its view of the quay, and the hour which they spend
together contribute to the scenic effect. But the language of space

after this—diving deep, touching bottom, soaring above or sinking below, and traveling far since the London theatre with Maria—is all metaphorical. It refers to the state of his consciousness and his awareness of his development since landing in Europe. The language of time—comparing past and present—also serves as an index of his consciousness. But the temporal comparisons provide only a surface perspective on consciousness; they relate it to a designated social time. The metaphoric phrase "travelled far since that evening in London" uses spatial language to provide a temporal perspective on the present afternoon in Paris. Strether's development is seen, then, as both a temporal progression and as a distance travelled. The metaphoric distance images the real distance between Woollett and Paris.

Simultaneity is an effect achieved by the overlap of spatial images. James uses this technique at least twice in the novel to show first how Strether's consciousness affects his perception and then the manner in which perception makes conscious the workings of the unconscious. At the theatre in London, Strether refuses to answer Maria's question about the unknown object. When she questions him again, we are told that "even for himself the picture of the stage was now overlaid with another image." To more serious effect simultaneity is achieved by the superimposition of Chad and Jeanne de Vionnet on Strether's perception of Gloriani. Through this effect Strether's unconscious admiration for Chad is subtly communicated. Strether realizes and then indicates to little Bilham that it is Chad he would enjoy being like. The scene demonstrates a turn of Strether's mind in Chad's favor: "What was clearest of all indeed was something much more than this, something at the single stroke of which—and wasn't it simply juxtaposition?—all vagueness vanished. It was the click of a spring—he saw the truth." To share the virtuous attachment with young Jeanne de Vionnet, Strether would be like Chad. And it is through the spatial juxtaposition of images that he is shown to experience this self-revelation.

The coupling of spatial and temporal elements is used also to indicate the distance between Woollett and Paris and to suggest the difference between the viewpoints of each. Thinking of the letters he writes to Woollett, Strether effects such a comparison:

> It was a great comfort to him in general not to have left
> past things to be dragged to light and explained; not to

> have to produce at so late a stage anything not produced, or anything even veiled and attenuated, at the moment. She knew it now: that was what he said to himself to-night in relation to the fresh fact of Chad's acquaintance with the two ladies—not to speak of the fresher one of his own. Mrs. Newsome knew in other words that very night at Woollett that he himself knew Madame de Vionnet and that he had conscientiously been to see her; also that he had found her remarkably attractive and that there would probably be a good deal more to tell. But she further knew, or would know very soon, that, again conscientiously, he hadn't repeated his visit.

Different perspectives are implied by the juxtaposition of Strether's activities and Mrs. Newsome's knowledge of them. Through his letters, Strether shares his knowledge with Mrs. Newsome, and their knowledge is now simultaneous. The difference between the two views is presented, then, through the spatial juxtaposition of the different perspectives. Though the parallel and contrast is accomplished through spatial relationships, it is further implied that that relationship is dependent upon time. It exists, that is, at a certain moment. Time is at once an attribute of spatial perspective and at the same time another kind of perspective itself.

Spatial perspective and temporal perspective are, of course, very different things. They are also radically different from the elements of spatial form and temporal form that we attempted to define earlier. Spatial and temporal forms are aspects of narrative technique and reflect an attitude toward time. Perspective deals with viewpoint. Because Strether held one view last month in Woollett and another this month in Paris does not mean that we are dealing with a temporal perspective. Rather, given the enormous difference between the views represented by the respective places, we are dealing with a primarily spatial perspective. But because Strether in himself changes—matures, or to follow the novel's imagery, ripens—we are also dealing with a perspective engendered by that change. It is a change effected in time and by time. The different perspectives result not so much from the trip to Europe—the Pococks make the same journey—but from the effect that Europe has upon Strether. That change obviously involves the repudiation of one viewpoint in favor of the other. But because we are "present at the process" of that change, we are not merely confronted with the result. And because in that process Strether discovers the possibilities latent in his earlier trip to Europe, both the process and the perspective are decidedly temporal. This does not mean that spatial perspective is to be disregarded, but rather that it is subordinated to the temporal "process of vision" that James held up as the novel's central and informing element.

Indeed, spatial perspective is used to confirm Strether's change. It is in light of his return to Woollett, he feels, that his development will prove most pronounced. Again, while contemplating his reckoning:

> It [the reckoning] was really behind everything; it hadn't merged in what he had done; his final appreciation of what he had done—his appreciation on the spot—would provide it with its main sharpness. The spot focused on was of course Woollett, and he was to see, at the best, what Woollett would be with everything there changed for him. Wouldn't *that* revelation practically amount to the wind-up of his career?

III. TIME AND DURATION

Poulet attributes the usually limited duration of the Jamesian character to the author's concern with primarily spatial rather than temporal perspectives. Though Strether, we have argued, is a special case, his duration is nevertheless limited in another way—through the attention which he must pay to social surfaces. This is reflected in the recurrent equation of the time-lapse required for mental process with the time-lapse required for the passage of social time. Though apprehension lags behind social time, and Strether does at times range rather freely, time does not stop while his mind is operating. In other words, if "past perfect retrospection" indicates that we are primarily interested in the workings of Strether's consciousness, it also indicates that social time continues while those workings are demonstrated. Strether becomes lost in an appreciation of Gloriani's person, for example, and we watch his mind operate through a long paragraph. Then our focus shifts to Chad's actions: "Chad meanwhile, after having easily named his companion, still more easily turned away." Chad's motions, though recorded after they have occurred, are placed on the same time scheme as Strether's thoughts. The use of *meanwhile* indicates that those thoughts bear the same relation to social time that Chad's actions do. This is not an isolated case. Continually Strether is recalled to social time in such a way as to indicate that social actions and the activities of consciousness are measured by the same gauge.

IV. Time and Value

The time in *The Ambassadors* is always ultimately the present. James's focus upon consciousness and his insistence upon dramatic scenes allows us to see a mind as it operates *now*. The narrative structure often introduces several layers of time which not only allow the exploration of the immediate past by observing Strether's consciousness, but also make present in the dramatic scenes a more significant body of information. The narrative time-sequence following little Bilham's declaration that Chad's is a virtuous attachment demonstrates both the establishment of the time in the present and the complexity of time-structures through which Strether attempts to come to terms with that declaration. At first we are told that he feels for the next few days as if he had a new lease on life. Not idle long, he soon imagines new problems. He takes them, along with news of Chad's insistence that he meet Madame de Vionnet and her daughter, to Maria. We are told that they discuss them "on the very next occasion of his seeing Maria Gostrey." Yet it turns out that he had already seen her the day after Bilham's announcement. The narrative then explores Strether's immediate reaction to the scene with Bilham. We move back to Maria's eventual grasp of what Bilham had said. Then we are back to the present dramatic scene— "this second occasion." Now the effect of this mistake we are led to make about "the very next occasion" leads us once again to realize that mental time and social time are equated. In other words, it is the very next occasion after his imagination had dealt with Bilham's revelation, not the next occasion after the revelation itself. The momentary flashbacks permit Strether a more-digested view of his own immediate reaction, while the foreshortening of the scene in which he relates Bilham's revelation to Maria gives the scene we are about to witness a greater dramatic density. It is the density with which Strether must always deal when confronting an immediately present problem. The present is always problematic, and social relations are always abrasive, elusive and volatile. Yet though dealing with the problematic present is initially forced upon him, Strether comes eventually to asseverate its value. The repudiation of his old past in favor of it is an essential movement of the novel.

Yet the present is given value beyond itself: all of the past is included in the present through the agency of memory. Memory is seen as both a value in itself and as proof of the value of a perception or experience. The meeting with Gloriani, clearly an important moment for Strether, is not only viewed through memory, its value is ascribed by the very fact that it is so intensely remembered. His response to Gloriani's face:

> He was to remember again repeatedly the medal-like Italian face, in which every line was an artist's own, in which time told only as tone and consecration; and he was to recall in especial, as the penetrating radiance, as the communication of the illustrious spirit itself, the manner in which, while they stood briefly, in welcome and response, face to face, he was held by the sculptor's eyes. He wasn't soon to forget them, was to think of them all unconscious . . . as the source of the deepest intellectual sounding to which he had ever been exposed. He was in fact quite to cherish his vision of it.

The value of his meeting with Gloriani and the significance of the impression upon Strether are affirmed by his remembrance of them. Memory, then, becomes a repository of value.

Late in the novel, memory is once again invoked as a proof of the depth and importance of Strether's transformation. The emphasis in the last few chapters upon the word *now*—it is several times italicized and occurs quite frequently in Strether's scenes with Madame de Vionnet, Maria, and Chad—indicates the importance of the present. The italics imply that the present is viewed in terms of the values which betoken Strether's transformation. The present contains the past and the accumulation of lessons and perspectives that the past has provided Strether. The present, then, has value not only in itself but also in the personal past contained in it. This personal past is accessible through memory.

And memory is to be for Strether a consolation. This is part of his logic in desiring to see Madame de Vionnet in her proper setting:

The objects about would help him, would really help them both. No, he might never see them again—this was only too probably the last time; and he should certainly see nothing in the least degree like them. He should soon be going to where such things were not, and it would be a small mercy for memory, for fancy, to have in that stress, a loaf on the shelf. He knew in advance he should look back on the perception actually sharpest with him as on the view of something old, old, old, the oldest thing he had ever personally touched; and he also knew, even while he took his companion in as the feature among features, that memory and fancy couldn't help being enlisted for her.

Then Madame de Vionnet is associated with her cultural past, and this, too, is to Strether part of the value of seeing her in her proper setting. "Tyrannies of history, facts of type," and "values of expression," all operate to place her in her cultural setting. The values of the past—personally and historically—are present to Strether in the person of Madame de Vionnet, and will remain so through his memory of her.

We need not here go into the attitude toward the historical past in the novel. It is enough to notice that for Strether the value is both in the past itself and in the process by which it has been transmitted from past to present; he admires the "spell of transmission" which he feels Madame de Vionnet to be under. The cultural past, and the traditions which have made it part of present culture form, of course, the values which Strether grows, through his perceptions, to appreciate.

But if he now values a newly-won appreciation of the cultural past of Europe, he also values the newly-wrought personal past which his contact with Europe has given him. Through the later chapters of the novel, Strether's memory becomes inhabited by the new past he has created for himself. He has learned to follow his own injunction to "live," and so creates through his intense appreciation of the present the material upon which his memory feeds. While Waymarsh now "somehow, seemed long ago," the memories which are current to Strether are not those of Woollett or even those of his first trip to Europe, but those which concern his present mission to Europe and the possibilities that it has helped him to retrieve. "He remembered everything," James tells us of Strether's interview with

Maria, "bringing up with humour even things of which she professed no recollection, things she vehemently denied; and falling back above all on the great interest of their early time, the curiosity felt by both of them as to where he would 'come out.' "

As part of the ironic reversal which E. M. Forster ascribes to the book's "pattern," Strether's old past becomes now his problematic future. While he is content with his memory of Europe and the richness of vision that his experience has awakened in him, he can express little confidence in the future. He accepts Madame de Vionnet's statement that nothing can help him now, and admits to Maria that he's different for Mrs. Newsome now that he sees her. He says to Maria that "there will always be something" to which he can go home; however, this is more to forestall Maria's questioning than to give an adequate assessment of his case.

The tragedy that Strether witnesses and tries to prevent—the tragedy of Madame de Vionnet—is his final lesson in the uncertainty and temporality of human affairs. It is she who makes him realize that the present and past have value, if only because of the uncertainty of the future. "There's not a grain of certainty in my future," she says, "for the only certainty is that I shall be a loser in the end." This could as well apply to Strether.

The Major Phase: *The Ambassadors*

Ronald Wallace

More has been written on *The Ambassadors,* perhaps, than on any other Jamesian novel. James himself left three extended "commentaries" on the book: the notebook "germ," the "project" for the novel which he sent to *Harper's,* and the preface. James considered the book "frankly, quite the best, 'all round,' of my productions," but he is characteristically ambiguous about its particular generic form. In the notebook entry he refers to the novel as "the whole comedy, or tragedy, the drama, whatever we call it."

Criticism has since called *The Ambassadors* many things, but few critics have called it predominantly comic, and only two essays have been devoted to the comedy of the novel. Floundering in generic uncertainty, critics have been unable to agree on the quality of Lambert Strether's education or the meaning of the conclusion of the novel. Does Strether learn everything or nothing, and if he learns anything, exactly what is it? Is the conclusion Strether's renunciation of all happiness and his return to the pathetic dominance of Mrs. Newsome, or is it positive affirmation, and if so, what does it affirm?

Such questions have interested critics since the novel was published, and the answers have been various. An early review in the *Nation* suggests that when Sarah Pocock arrives in Paris to replace Strether as ambassador she "sweeps the cobwebs from Strether's brain. . . . he was inevitably and by the nature of things committed

From *Henry James and the Comic Form.* © 1975 by the University of Michigan. University of Michigan Press, 1975.

to Woollett." E. M. Forster observes that the "rigid pattern" of the novel "shuts the door on life and leaves the novelist doing exercises, generally in the drawing-room." Even F. O. Matthiessen in his perceptive study of "the major phase" complains that although Strether has awakened to a new sense of life by the end "he does nothing at all to fulfill that sense. . . . we cannot help feeling his relative emptiness." And more recently Robert E. Garis has argued that Strether's vision in the French countryside "produces . . . a sickening sequence of acts and attitudes devoid of imaginative energy but at the time depressingly agile in both romantic and moralistic self-deception—produces, in brief, final evidence of Strether's incapacity for either education or life."

Strether's education, his capacity for life, and his self-awareness present the most important questions in the book, and no answers which ignore the genre of the novel can approach validity. The remarkable organic concision and the dramatic and scenic unity make an understanding of the form of the novel indispensable to a clear understanding of Strether's final vision. Leon Edel suggests the proper approach when he describes *The Ambassadors* as a "trans-Atlantic comedy of manners." "And like all great comedies, it treated of matters grave as well as gay." The form of the novel is that of comedy, and Strether's final vision is the highest comic vision available to the form.

The Ambassadors is the late novel which owes most to the comedy of manners form. Chad, upon inheriting his money, has gone to the bad; that is, to Paris. Mrs. Newsome, sitting on the remainder of the family fortune, is divided between the dread that Chad will marry the Parisian strumpet with whom he lives, which will be awful, and the fear that he will merely continue to live with her, which will be worse. In pursuit of the decadent son, Strether is like the typical country visitor who comes to the city and is seduced by its ways into exchanging a morally staid life for a more sensuous and intellectually rich one. In his role as Mrs. Newsome's emissary, Strether is also the typical blocking figure, exerting paternal power to separate two lovers. As in James's earlier parody romance, *The Spoils of Poynton, The Ambassadors* is told from the blocking figure's point of view. But in this novel the blocking figure is converted.

The other characters also are reminiscent of the conventional social types from the comedy of manners: the man of the world, the *jeune fille,* the *femme du monde,* the great artist, the young rake, and the deceived husband. By contrast to Strether the other players are, as Richard Chase observes, "the fools, gulls, and fops of the stage comedies."

As in James's earlier comedies of manners, the opposing societies or conflicting sensibilities which produce the drama are America and Europe, here symbolized by Woollett and Paris. The conflict is not, however, as simple as Stephen Spender implies when he concludes that "Paris is life. Woollett is death." Woollett does seem rigid, inflexible, and parochial while Paris seems relaxed, flexible, and cosmopolitan. But, as in the earlier novels, both societies represent potential for both good and evil. Strether's character reflects the America James loved, and Madame de Vionnet's suffering reflects the dangers of European manner and sensibility.

Nevertheless, the novel is structured partly on the polarity of Woollett and Paris, and Woollett is obviously the negative pole. In Woollett, individual identity is determined by names on the covers of green reviews or by marriage to prominent persons. When Maria Gostrey asks Strether who Jim Pocock is, Strether replies, "Why Sally's husband. That's the only way we distinguish people at Woollett." Strether himself has led the life of a nonentity.

In Woollett, productivity is another form of identity and there is something positively unpleasant or embarrassing about leisure. As Strether tells Maria, "Woollett isn't sure it ought to enjoy." Woollett's moral strictures and puritan frame of mind prevent it from finding "amusement," a quality upon which James repeatedly insisted. Strether reveals that although "there were opinions at Woollett," they are on "only three or four" subjects, and people are ashamed of them. In Paris, however, Strether discovers that opinions are a prime aspect of enjoyment and are actually cultivated and made the basis of personal relationship.

Finally, despite its moral intensity and concern with the future, Woollett has no positive conception of the end toward which it so strenuously moves. The little unnamed article which symbolizes all of Chad's future and all of the Newsomes' dreams is "a small, trivial, rather ridiculous object of commonest domestic use." It is even too vulgar for Strether to hazard naming it. And yet Strether, speaking as Mrs. Newsome's emissary, mechanically affirms that it is "a big brave bouncing business. A roaring trade . . . a great production, a great industry." All of Woollett's moral energy is centered on this object, and it becomes the real reason for Strether's mission to retrieve Chad who will become advertising manager.

Paris, on the other hand, is "a jewel brilliant and hard," and James choses it as an antithesis to Woollett from among the cities of Europe because "There was the dreadful little old tradition, one of the platitudes of the human comedy, that people's moral scheme *does* break down in Paris." Although Paris lacks the creative moral possibility of Woollett, it also lacks the repressive moral vigor. And Parisian society cultivates leisure and amusement, delighting in the ambiguities of human behavior.

Both cities, therefore, represent for Strether and for James attitudes which are valuable and dangerous. If Woollett is narrow and unimaginative it also represents a beautiful devotion to principle and morality. If Paris is the capacity to enjoy and expand awareness, it also represents appearance and cynicism. But, as Leon Edel observes, Europe is "the very touchstone of the novel" and the comic action arises largely from the conflict between characters who see life from the narrow perspective of Woollett or from the larger perspective of Paris.

As the title suggests, James presents the movement from Woollett to Paris in the humorous terms of the mock-heroic, just as he had previously imaged the conflict over the "spoils" of Poynton. Throughout the novel Strether's affair is treated as a diplomatic mission, and the language and strategy of diplomacy are constantly evident. Strether's first private meeting with Madame de Vionnet reads like the transcript of an initial meeting between two representatives of opposing governments negotiating a peace. Marie begins:

> "I don't think you seriously believe in what you're doing," she said; "but all the same, you know, I'm going to treat you quite as if I did."
>
> "By which you mean," Strether directly replied, "quite as if you didn't! I assure you it won't make the least difference with me how you treat me."
>
> "Well," she said, taking that menace bravely and philosophically enough, "the only thing that really matters is that you shall get on with me."
>
> "Ah but I don't!" he immediately returned.
>
> It gave her another pause; which, however, she happily

enough shook off. "Will you consent to go on with me a little—provisionally—as if you did?"

The polite verbal battle, the initial diplomatic amenities, the jockeying for position, and final establishment of a compromise base for relations all suggest conscious parody of the ambassadorial role which Strether has assumed.

James adds to the mock-heroic tone by doubling the American ambassadors in Paris, sending a new deputation led by Sarah Pocock. Whereas Strether had originally come to Paris to rescue Chad, now the Pococks come to Paris to rescue Chad and Strether. As spokesman for "the deputation from Woollett" Sarah Pocock uses the ambassadorial "we." She tells Strether, "You're right, we haven't quite known what you mean, Mother and I, but now we see Chad's magnificent." Strether feels "like the outgoing ambassador . . . doing honor to his appointed successor."

The Pococks, in their moral rigidity and lack of response to "Europe," are a comic parody of Strether's earlier response to his new surroundings. Having himself been "effectively bribed," he wonders whether Sarah is likewise bribable, and in his shifted position he regards her as "the enemy." His strategy for revealing to the Pococks his questionable relationship with Maria Gostrey is "a conception of carrying the war into the enemy's country by showing surprise at the enemy's ignorance." Strether ironically becomes Chad's and his own ambassador, negotiating with the enemy Pococks.

But if the Pococks parody Strether's mission, they also force him to review his understanding of his situation. Upon their arrival he wonders:

> Was he, on this question of Chad's improvement, fantastic and away from the truth? Did he live in a false world. . . . Was this contribution of the real possibly the mission of the Pococks?—had they come to make the work of observation, as *he* had practiced observation, crack and crumble. . . . Had they come in short to be sane where Strether was destined to feel that he himself had only been silly?

James had examined the possibilities of the ultimate insanity of the creative mind in *The Sacred Fount*. But, unlike the narrator of that novel, Strether shares a community of love and relationship with his new European allies, and his approach to life is positive and compassionate. Strether survives the test of seeing his own earlier self parodied in the Pococks, and wonders whether it would not make "more for reality to be silly with these persons [Chad, Marie, and Maria] than sane with Sarah and Jim."

Finally, the Pococks serve the additional comic function of providing the occasion for doubling and tripling both ambassadors and "virtuous attachments." In his notebook outline James recognizes the rich comic possibilities of the Pococks' arrival. He catalogues the potential relationships: "The Vionnets and the Pococks, Chad and his sister, Pocock and his brother-in-law, Chad and Pocock's sister, Strether and Pocock, Pocock and Strether, Strether and everyone and everything, but Strether and Mrs. Pocock in especial."

When Strether first arrives in Paris as Mrs. Newsome's ambassador, Maria Gostrey observes that little Bilham is Chad's ambassador, getting daily communiqués from Cannes. She perceives that the seemingly accidental meeting of little Bilham and Strether at Chad's apartment has been carefully and artfully planned. After meeting Chad and Madame de Vionnet, Strether thinks that Madame de Vionnet will be Chad's new ambassador, but he soon learns that Chad is ambassador for Madame de Vionnet. Again Maria Gostrey interprets the situation correctly. "I dare say you're right . . . about Mr. Newsome's little plan. He *has* been trying you—has been reporting on you to these friends." If the American ambassadors are comically doubled, the European ambassadors are tripled.

The "virtuous attachments" also receive the same treatment. Upon meeting the Vionnets, Strether assumes that little Jeanne is Chad's virtuous attachment, but later learns that Madame de Vionnet herself fills the role. Strether has already formed his own "virtuous attachment" with Maria Gostrey, and the advent of the Pococks forces him self-consciously to justify his friendship with her. When Marie mentions Maria to Sarah, Strether abruptly and somewhat nervously counters:

> "Oh yes indeed . . . Mrs. Pocock knows about Miss Gostrey. Your mother, Sarah, must have told you about her; your mother knows everything," he sturdily pursued. "And I cordially admit," he added with his conscious

gaiety of courage, "that she's as wonderful a woman as you like."

Suspicious Sarah Pocock replies dryly that she knows nothing about Maria Gostrey.

Thus Strether, who goes to Paris to rescue Chad from a "virtuous attachment," forms one of his own. And when Sarah comes to rescue Chad and Strether, she herself forms a "virtuous attachment" with Waymarsh and goes off on a trip to Switzerland. Again Maria Gostrey perceives the situation. Strether asks her about Sarah, "You mean she has fallen in love?" and Maria replies, "I mean she wonders if she hasn't—and it serves all her purpose."

Finally, Jim Pocock, Waymarsh, and Chad all reflect aspects of Strether and partially serve, like Sarah Pocock, as parodic copies of him. In his notebook James suggests that Jim Pocock "is an example, in characteristically vulgar form, and with all due humorous effect, of the same 'fatal' effect of European opportunities on characters giving way too freely, which Strether more subtly embodies." Jim's enthusiastic response to Europe and the magnificent "varieties" is the "type" response of a tourist in Paris who immediately wants to see all the girlie shows. And Strether perceives his own potential similarity to Pocock. "Might it even become the same should he marry in a few months?" Pocock represents a picture of what would be in store for Strether as Mrs. Newsome's husband.

Waymarsh is another aspect of Strether. As the "conscience of Milrose" he represents Strether's American morality and suspicion of amusement and leisure. But Strether refuses to allow the "humor" aspect of his own character to prevail, and Waymarsh is partially converted in the end.

Strether's relationship to Chad, however, provides the situation for the most obvious comic "turn" in the novel. Just when Chad is ready to agree to return to Woollett, Strether decides that he must stay. Chad is incredulous and Strether asks (as Chad had earlier) that the young man have patience with him and give him time. Chad asks, "You want me now to 'stay?' " and James comments:

> The change of position and of relation, for each, was so oddly betrayed in the question that Chad laughed out as soon as he had uttered it—which made Strether also laugh.

James emphasizes this comic reversal of roles when he reveals Strether's fear that Chad will misinterpret Strether's "virtuous attachment" to Maria Gostrey and write home to Mrs. Newsome about it. Although Strether is supposed to judge Chad's misbehavior, he worries that Chad will judge his. The juxtaposition of a youthful but sophisticated Chad with the mature but innocent and gullible Strether is itself comic.

The structure of the novel, then, with its opposition of conflicting societies, its mock-heroic tone, and its doublings and triplings is that of the comedy of manners. Within this framework Lambert Strether progresses slowly toward a great comic ironic vision. Indeed, his final vision is the central focus of the novel, and the steps in his education are important in fully understanding the nature of his ultimate insight.

F. W. Dupee suggests that at the beginning of the novel Strether displays the "kind [of innocence] usually reserved for the fools or dupes of comedy." The American innocent, faced with more things than Woollett has ever dreamed of in its philosophy, will, nevertheless, be educated by his European experience toward full, mature wisdom. By the end of the novel Strether has gained a perspective on himself and his situation, on morality and beauty, which places him above any other Jamesian protagonist. James had expressed doubt about making any fictional character too finely aware. But Strether's awareness at the close, an awareness based on an understanding of his previous ignorance, approaches omniscience.

Ian Watt observes that James's attitude toward Strether at the outset is "humorous." Strether arrives at Liverpool sporting his "perpetual pair of glasses" and is rather too pleased in his discovery that Waymarsh has not yet arrived. In the first paragraph Strether reveals his concern for Waymarsh, his love of Waymarsh, and his relief that he doesn't have to see Waymarsh just yet. Strether is a conscientious friend who would feel guilty if anyone, including himself, knew that he was less than anxious to meet an old friend immediately. James couches Strether's thoughts in negative hyperbole, exposing Strether's desire to fool himself. Strether is "not wholly disconcerted" by Waymarsh's absence but he does "not absolutely . . . desire" his presence, and he happily laments the fact that he will have to "postpone for a few hours the enjoyment of" Waymarsh's company. He bravely tells himself that he can "wait without disappointment." Strether's pleasure is revealed through the language of disappointment, and his efforts to fool himself relate him unmistakably to the gull of traditional comedy.

But if Strether's self-deception is slightly comic at the outset, he appreciates the human necessity of forms. He considers it his duty to make Waymarsh believe that he is anxious to see him, and when he does meet Waymarsh he feigns absolute delight. At the beginning of the novel Strether already knows what it takes Maggie Verver so long to learn: the value of manners in personal relationships. The important knowledge Strether must gain is wholly different.

Part of Strether's problem from the beginning is his rigid adherence to Woollett morality, symbolized by his desire to formulate and categorize his experience in Europe. Like the humors of traditional comedy, Strether wants formulation rather than freedom. James suggests in the preface that "the false position for him, I say, was obviously to have presented himself at the gate of that boundless menagerie primed with a moral scheme of the most approved pattern which was yet framed to break down on any approach to vivid facts."

Strether admits that "what he wanted was some idea that would simplify" and he grasps at any formula which might help him to understand Chad. On first meeting Chad, Strether quickly types him as "a man of the world—a formula that indeed seemed to come now in some degree to his relief." But Strether's initial formula is abruptly overturned and Strether substitutes another equally erroneous label: "he asked himself if he weren't perhaps really dealing with an irreducible young Pagan." Since a pagan is "the thing most wanted at Woollett" Strether jumps at this idea. If Chad is indeed a pagan, he has been made so by a malign influence and is in need of rescue. As the problem begins to reveal its complexity Strether continues to search for an easy and moralistic way out. Late in volume 1 "he failed quite to see how his situation could clear up at all logically except by some turn of events that would give him the pretext of disgust."

Strether's initial education is a moral education. All his Woollett categories are destined to failure because they distort reality. Strether's first great moment of awareness comes, of course, in Gloriani's garden where he realizes that Woollett's morality at its worst is narrow and restrictive, and ultimately destructive to any creative living. At this point in his education Strether has given up his moral sense altogether, or so he thinks, and his famous advice to little Bilham is a great amoral tribute to life.

James affirms in the preface that Strether's speech to little Bilham is the "essence" of the novel. "Live all you can; it's a mistake not to." And later in the novel when little Bilham reverts to the advice, "Didn't you adjure me . . . to see?" Strether fails to correct him. Living and seeing, consciousness and awareness, are the thematic heart of the novel. But if at this moment in Gloriani's garden Strether can affirm the necessity of living and seeing, he does not yet himself possess the full comic vision. Two subsequent painful experiences are required to impress upon Strether the consequences of his advice to little Bilham.

Strether, weary of his ambassadorial responsibilities, journeys alone into the French countryside and comes upon a scene which recalls a Lambinet painting he had once thought of buying. As he steps into the Lambinet frame he sees "exactly the right thing" to complete the picture: "two very happy persons" floating down the river in a boat. But when he perceives that the couple in the boat is actually Marie and Chad, he experiences the ritual death typical of comedy and becomes sick to "his spiritual stomach." But James does not emphasize his disillusionment so much as he does Strether's struggle to make it right, to incorporate a broader vision of "life" into the Lambinet. Realizing that he is not "in Madame de Vionnet's boat," Strether quickly regains his balance and hails the couple loudly. What he learns through this experience is that "intimacy, at such a point, was *like* that—and what in the world else would one have wished it to be like?" He finds himself "supposing innumerable and wonderful things," for the intimacy is such a "vivid illustration of his famous knowing how to live."

But Strether does not fully appreciate the difference his new knowledge makes for himself until later. It is in the telegraph office on the following day that Strether attains a full comic vision which reconciles human ideality with human limitation, human morality with human passion. Glancing around at the bustling life in the *Postes et Télégraphes,* Strether realizes that "He was mixed up with the typical tale of Paris, and so were they, poor things—how could they all together help being? They were no worse than he, in short, and he no worse than they—if, queerly enough, no better."

Meredith writes that comedy "enfolds characters with the wretched host of the world, huddles them with us all in an ignoble assimilation," and Louis Kronenberger defines the comic vision as "the evidence that we are no better than other people, and . . . the knowledge that most other people are no better than we are. It makes us more critical but it leaves us more tolerant." Wylie Sypher observes that the comic recognition that one is a fool is the "moral perception that competes with tragic recognition." Throughout the novel Strether had hesitantly and uncertainly moved toward this moral perception. Early in the book he wondered "Were there then sides on which his predicament threatened to look rather droll to him?" and he suspected that he "carried himself like a fool." In his adjuration to little Bilham in Gloriani's garden he had expounded on the limitations inherent in freedom. Life is, he affirmed, "at the best a tin mould . . . into which, a helpless jelly, one's consciousness is poured. . . . Still, one has the illusion of freedom." What Strether experiences in the telegraph office is the illusory quality of his superiority and his freedom. Like everyone else he is imperfect and limited.

And yet, despite the sobering knowledge, Strether resiliently rebounds to affirm the beauty of the whole situation and his precious fallibility. Unlike Christopher Newman, *The Sacred Fount* narrator, or Isabel Archer before him, Strether completely accepts the awareness of his innate comicality while asserting the ever present possibilities of life. Earlier "he had seemed to wince at the amount of comedy involved; whereas in his present posture he could only ask himself how he should enjoy any attempt from her [Marie] to take the comedy back. He shouldn't enjoy it at all." And he sees himself as "the droll mixture . . . of his braveries and fears, the general spectacle of his art and his innocence."

Strether achieves what Hegel calls "the happy frame of mind, a hale condition of soul, which, fully aware of itself, can suffer the dissolution of its aims and realization." Or in Meredith's terms he has been "able to detect the ridicule of them you love without loving them less; and . . . able to see yourself somewhat ridiculous in dear eyes, and accepting the correction their image of you proposes." Strether discovers his own lack of moral superiority as well as the inadequacy of the moral views of either Woollett or Paris. His illusions and pretensions are squared with reality and he sees the beauty of his situation. "The work, however admirable, was nevertheless of the strict human order, and in short it was marvelous that the companion of mere earthly joys, of comforts, aberrations (however one classed them) within the common experience, should be so transcendently prized." At the height of vision Strether is able to see Madame de Vionnet as both "the finest and subtlest creature" and as "a maidservant crying for her young man."

The final dialogue with Maria Gostrey is probably the most misinterpreted passage in all of James. Richard Chase, who has written on the comedy in the novel, complains that the rejection of Miss Gostrey is "another one of those all too gratuitous renunciations that James prizes so highly." F. O. Matthiessen feels that Strether "leaves Paris and Maria to go back to no prospect of life at all." And Yvor Winters claims it is a "sacrifice of morality to appearances."

But to see the end of the novel as tragic renunciation is to misread both Strether's vision and the form of the book. Within the comic structure Maria Gostrey is merely the comic confidante described in chapter 3. James insists in the preface that Maria is "the reader's friend much rather" than Strether's "and she acts in that capacity, and *really* in that capacity alone." She "has nothing to do with the matter . . . but has everything to do with the manner" of the novel. To feel sorry for Miss Gostrey is to forget that she is not really part of the "matter" of the book.

Strether's final dialogue with Maria is far from renunciation, unless it be the renunciation of a return to narrower vision. Maria asks,

> "To what do you go home?"
> "I don't know. There will always be something."
> "To a great difference," she said as she kept his hand.
> "A great difference—no doubt. Yet I shall see what I can make of it."

She sighed it at last all comically, all tragically, away.

The tragedy is Miss Gostrey's, the comedy is Strether's. With the voice of the true high comic hero he vows to "see what I can make of it." James interprets the conclusion clearly in his preface:

> He *can't* accept or assent. He won't. . . . He has come so far through his total little experience that he has come out on the other side—on the other side even, of a union with Miss Gostrey. He must go back as he came—or rather, really, so quite other that, in comparison, marrying Miss

Gostrey would be almost of the old order. Yes, he goes back other—and to other things.

In his brilliant essay on comedy Wylie Sypher describes the comic vision in terms that summarize Strether's awareness and recall the final sentence of *The Ambassadors*.

> At its most triumphant moments comic art frees us from peril without destroying our ideals. . . . Comedy can be a means of mastering our disillusions when we are caught in a dishonest or stupid society. . . . We see the flaws in things, but we do not always need to concede the victory. . . . Unflinching and undaunted we see *where we are*.
>
> ("Meanings of Comedy")

It is no accident that Strether's final words in the novel affirm his vision: "Then there we are."

If Strether's ultimate recognition seems too sophisticated and profound for a comedy of manners, that is because *The Ambassadors* is not a typical comedy of manners. Beneath the conventional frame lies a deeper kind of comedy which floats the whole into the realm of mythic experience.

Austen Warren suggests the mythic shape of *The Ambassadors* when he remarks that "In poetic drama—*The Tempest* . . . James came nearest to finding precedents for his later novels." A number of striking similarities between the two masterpieces reveal them to be of a similar archetypal structure and meaning.

In many ways Strether is the Prospero of *The Ambassadors,* creating the entire action of the plot out of his own mind. At the outset he seems more like the inverted Prospero of *The Sacred Fount,* comically ignorant but desiring to control the action. Strether uses his magic innocence and creativity to create the illusions he sees. Madame de Vionnet's apartment, for example, "was doubtless half the projection of his mind." In the Lambinet frame he feels that he is able "sufficiently [to] command the scene" and he "quite recalled . . . conjuring away everything but the pleasant." Part of what Strether must ultimately learn is that his conjurings have created visions of baseless fabric. Strether finally discovers that he has been a fool all along, and, at the close, he perceives that the real is no less wonderful than the imaginary.

Landing on his island, Strether encounters a Caliban in Waymarsh. As lovable as Waymarsh may be, Strether is not overly excited to see him, for Waymarsh has not been able to adjust to Europe. He complains, "It ain't my kind of a country." Like Caliban, he is humorless and unmannered, and he exerts a depressing influence on Strether.

As Waymarsh is superficially a Caliban, Maria Gostrey is an Ariel, an imaginative and creative spirit, who pulls Strether up whereas Waymarsh drags him down. Maria's magic is revealed in her incredible clairvoyance. When Strether meets her "She knew even intimate things about him that he hadn't yet told her." And when Strether asks her to teach him to "enjoy," she asks, "Is it really an 'order' from you?—that I shall take the job?" Maria is responsible for much of Strether's power of awareness and even for his mobility in Europe. At one point he finds himself "by Miss Gostrey's side at one of the theatres to which he had found himself transported, without his own hand raised, or the mere expression of a conscientious wonder." Indisputably magical, Miss Gostrey provides Strether with knowledge and perception.

Like Waymarsh, Chad seems to be a Caliban at the outset, a creature "under a spell, a blight, a dark and baffling influence," and Strether expects to find him a "brute." But this Caliban's nature has been improved by the nurture of a Miranda, and Strether immediately succumbs to Chad's charm, now mistaking him for a Ferdinand. At the close, however, when Chad expresses interest in "Advertising scientifically worked," it appears that he is reverting to his Caliban role, and Strether repeats to Chad that if he leaves Marie he is a "beast."

The conflicting societies of *The Ambassadors* also resemble those of *The Tempest*. Like Prospero, Strether is exiled from one society to another. Like Milan, Woollett is the world of crass, petty, and selfish affairs, and, like the island, Paris is a land of magic, freedom, and beauty. But Prospero's island is in many ways inferior to Milan, just as Paris is to Woollett. There are fens and marshes as well as beautiful music on the island, and human possibility is limited. The only love available to Miranda is that of her father. Strether finds Europe a land of enchantment but learns that enchantment can veil evil and suffering.

Finally, Strether and several of the other characters are, like the characters in *The Tempest,* shipwrecked. At the outset James refers to "poor Lambert Strether washed up on the sunny strand." Soon thereafter Strether notes that little Bilham "hadn't saved from his shipwreck a scrap of anything but his beautiful intelligence." Both Prospero and Strether cause their relatives to shipwreck on their magic island, and when Strether sees Mamie Pocock on Chad's balcony he "fancied himself stranded with her on a far shore, during an ominous calm, in a quaint community of shipwreck."

The Ambassadors, then, resembles *The Tempest.* Banished to a magic island, Strether encounters a Caliban, an Ariel, and a pair of lovers, and forces the arrival of his relatives from the humorous society that sent him off originally. The parallels are, of course, somewhat superficial, for as James himself wrote in his essay on *The Tempest,* "any story will provide a remote island, a shipwreck and a coincidence." But the underlying archetypal structure of the stories is, perhaps, more significant.

Both the novel and the play are, in shape, displacement stories. In a displacement story the action often begins in a normal world, moves into the green world where a metamorphosis and a comic resolution is achieved, and returns to the normal world. The hero is thus displaced from his ordinary sense of reality into an illusory dreamland, but his very displacement gives him a perspective on himself that enables him to return to the normal world renewed.

Strether is physically, intellectually, emotionally, and morally displaced before attaining the self-knowledge and renewed affirmation of life with which he returns to Woollett. His journey is much more than that from Woollett to Paris. At the outset he has the "sense of himself as at that moment launched in something of which the sense would be quite disconnected from the sense of his past." And later he suffers "the queer displacement of his point of view." In his disarranging adventure the hero is removed from the familiar real world into a strange and hostile, if beautiful, universe in which ordinary names don't fit and easy categories break down.

Europe disarranges Strether's intellectual and emotional balance, and the journey into the Lambinet painting disarranges Strether's moral balance. Back in the real world of the telegraph office, among other merely human people, Strether is able to reconcile the ideality of his vision with the reality of its collapse. But his experience implies no resignation; he has had his vision, and the life he returns to, as James tells us, will be "other"; he will "make something of it."

At the end of *The Tempest* Prospero acknowledges "this thing of darkness," Caliban, to be his, forgives his enemies, drowns his book, and returns to human responsibility in Milan where he had previously dedicated himself to the study of magic rather than to his people. He frees Ariel and returns to a world transformed only by love.

Strether's knowledge follows a similar pattern. Having been displaced in the enchanted world of Europe, Strether recognizes the reality and illusion of both worlds, acknowledges his responsibility in the Chad–Marie affair, and returns to new life in Woollett where he had been previously without identity. Strether's recognition of his common humanity in the telegraph office is Prospero's recognition of Caliban. And Strether's farewell to Maria is Prospero's freeing of Ariel. Strether sees Maria as "the offer of exquisite service, of lightened care, for the rest of his days." Yet "to be right" he leaves without her. He no longer needs her magic, and indeed to accept it would be to deny his vision. By importuning Chad to remain with Marie, and by leaving Europe himself, Strether gives up all claim to perpetual care from either Mrs. Newsome or Maria Gostrey. To give up magic is to take a chance on human failure, but the reward of the chance is "life."

James had prepared himself for the creation of Strether in his creation of Christopher Newman, the narrator of *The Sacred Fount,* and Longdon; but the form of *The Ambassadors* and the depth of Strether's vision surpass the form and vision of any of the earlier novels. A subtle combination of international comedy of manners and archetypal displacement myth, *The Ambassadors* is James's masterpiece as *The Tempest* was Shakespeare's. James wrote to Hugh Walpole in humorous terms:

> I remember sitting on it, when I wrote it, with that intending weight and presence with which you probably often sit in these days on your trunk to make the lid close and *all* your trousers and boots go in.

Like *The Tempest, The Ambassadors* seems a composite of its author's productions, pulsing with all his sense of the tragedy and comedy of life. James's comedy of manners was to appear again in E. M. Forster's first novel, *Where Angels Fear to Tread,* a novel which closely parallels the plot and structure of *The Ambassadors,* and James's mythic comedy was to appear again in James Joyce's *Ulysses,* a novel in which another father searches for his son. But no novelist was again to produce the peculiar fusion of forms; it was James's alone.

James: The Logic of Intensity— "Almost Socratic"

Martin Price

As James presents one of Mrs. Brookenham's questions, he calls her "almost Socratic." It is an interesting observation because one feels at times a remote influence upon James of the Platonic dialogues. I have no wish to fix that influence but only to consider the kind of midwifery of ideas, like that which Socrates claims, we can find in some of James's dialogue. One of the forms of intensity James achieves is the dramatization of a process wherein a man's accepted ideas are gradually brought into question and replaced. A good instance [in *The Ambassadors*] is the evening Lambert Strether spends in London with Maria Gostrey, at dinner and at the theater. It is also a good instance of that principle of which James wrote to H. G. Wells: "It is art that *makes* life, makes interest, makes importance."

In this chapter, the first of book 2, Strether is learning "to find names" for many matters, and on no evening of his life has he tried to supply so many. Maria Gostrey is the "mistress of a hundred cases or categories," and Strether soon feels that she "knew even intimate things about him that he hadn't yet told her and perhaps never would." She is eliciting from him the names or categories by which he has organized experience all of his life in America, and the very process by which she elicits them requires Strether to bring them to full consciousness, and then withdraw from, circumambulate, and question attitudes he has so far taken as natural and necessary. He has

From *Forms of Life: Character and Moral Development in the Novel.* © 1983 by Yale University. Yale University Press, 1983.

not told her these things about himself because he has not known that he knew them. They emerge in consciousness through the art of her questions.

Everything about Strether's evening defines itself in opposition to the world he has known; when he has gone to the theater with his American patron, Mrs. Newsome, he has enjoyed no "little confronted dinner, no pink lights, no whiff of vague sweetness." Nor has Mrs. Newsome ever worn a dress cut so low. Strether finds himself given over to "uncontrolled perception," to a freedom of awareness that Mrs. Newsome's black dress and white ruff have never encouraged. The red velvet band around Maria's throat becomes a "starting-point for fresh backward, fresh forward, fresh lateral flights." If Mrs. Newsome's ruff suggested Queen Elizabeth, Maria Gostrey's band evokes Mary Stuart. Strether finds in himself a "candor of fancy" that takes pleasure in such an antithesis. The texture of all he sees becomes more complex; the English "types" both on the stage and in the audience will prove more varied and distinct than Woollett allowed.

As Maria Gostrey draws Strether out on the subject of his mission, she requires him to attend to those terms he has never before questioned. She often echoes a response, holding a note he has sounded until it becomes the object of their joint perception. And to see with her eyes is to begin to free himself from the limits in which he has unconsciously acquiesced. She has also a tendency to abet his most treasonous thoughts. He begins, at the theater, to feel "kindness" for the young man on the stage who wears perpetual evening dress and weakly succumbs to "a bad woman in a yellow frock." Would Chad Newsome (whom he has come to rescue) wear evening dress, too? Would Strether have to do so himself to meet Chad at a proper level?

As his own thoughts warily approach such questions, Maria Gostrey puts them so directly before him that he can hardly evade them. "You've accepted the mission of separating him from the wicked woman. Are you quite sure she's very bad for him?" Strether is startled by the question: "Of course we are. Wouldn't *you* be?" Maria refuses the comfort of easy judgment. "One can only judge the facts." Might, after all, the woman be charming? Again, Strether is startled:

> "Charming?"—Strether stared before him. "She's base, venal—out of the streets."

> "I see. And *he—?*"
> "Chad, wretched boy?"
> "Of what type and temper is he?" she went on as
> Strether had lapsed.

We aren't told why he has "lapsed," but presumably he is forced to ask himself whether Chad is merely a virtuous American lad seduced.

> "Well—the obstinate." It was as if for a moment he had
> been going to say more and had then controlled himself.
> That was scarce what she wanted. "Do you like him?"
> This time he was prompt. "No. How *can* I?"

Once Strether has acknowledged his dislike of Chad Newsome, he wishes to attribute it to the son's treatment of his mother. Mrs. Newsome inspires a rather exalted idiom: "He has darkened her admirable life." Then, as if to bring it down to earth, Strether makes the point less stuffily: "He has worried her half to death." Maria, for reasons of her own, picks up the first and, as it were, the "official" version: "Is her life very admirable?" To this Strether replies with a solemn, perhaps reverent, "Extraordinarily." James indicates the timing of these remarks: "There was so much in the tone that Miss Gostrey had to devote another pause to the appreciation of it." She proceeds to deflate Strether's dictum and perhaps also to uncover the strong managerial role of Mrs. Newsome: "And he has only *her?* I don't mean the bad woman in Paris . . . for I assure you I shouldn't even at the best be disposed to allow him more than one. But has he only his mother?"

Strether mentions Chad's sister, Sarah Pocock, and he can imply of her, as he could not of her mother, that she is not universally beloved. Maria calls up Strether's earlier "admirable": "But *you* admire her?" And this releases Strether's critical awareness: "I'm perhaps a little afraid of her." What Maria is trying to uncover is the kind of will that governs the ladies and Strether as their ambassador. When he exclaims that they would do "anything in the world for him," Maria turns that conventional tribute inside out: "And you'd do anything in the world for them?" Strether is uncomfortable; she "had made it perhaps just a shade too affirmative for his nerves: 'Oh I don't know.' " Their generosity begins to turn, under Maria's cool queries, into something like officiousness. "The 'anything' they'd do is represented by their *making* you do it."

A comic view of Mrs. Newsome begins to emerge. "She puts so much of herself into everything—." And Maria nicely picks up the absurdity: "that she has nothing left for anything else?" Strether begins to let go his admiration. Maria supposes that "if your friend *had* come she would take great views, and the great views, to put it simply, would be too much for her." Strether by now is no longer defensive; he is "amused at" Maria's "notion of the simple," but accepts her terms: "Everything's too much for her."

James catches the conflict of exaltation and vulgarity in the unmentionable thing whose manufacture is the source of Mrs. Newsome's wealth: "a small trivial, rather ridiculous object of the commonest domestic use," Strether lamely describes it; "it's rather wanting in—what shall I say? Well, dignity, or the least approach to distinction." James looks ahead to Maria's many attempts to have him name it; with their failure she can treat "the little nameless object as indeed unnameable—she could make their abstention enormously definite." And behind this suppressed object there are sources of money even more questionable, not simply vulgar but dishonest. We begin to see Mrs. Newsome covering these wrongs with a high manner, as a "moral swell," the patron of the review that Strether edits and that few read. "It's her tribute to the ideal," Strether explains. Maria puts it otherwise: "You assist her to expiate—which is rather hard when you've yourself not sinned."

Perhaps the saddest and most significant exchange concerns the plans for Chad:

> "He stands . . . if you succeed with him, to gain—"
>
> "Oh a lot of advantages." Strether had them clearly at his fingers' ends.
>
> "By which you mean of course a lot of money."
>
> "Well, not only. I'm acting with a sense for him of other things too. Consideration and comfort and security—the general safety of being anchored by a strong chain. He wants, as I see him, to be protected. Protected I mean from life."
>
> "Ah *voilà!*"—her thought fitted with a click. "From life. What you *really* want to get him home for is to marry him."

There is something pitiable in this distrust of "life." Strether has been, as he now would have Chad be, "anchored by a strong chain." To question this prepares, of course, for his speech in Gloriani's garden, the rueful "Live all you can!"

Maria Gostrey has come to recognize the range of awareness that Strether can, with release, attain. He has modesty, simplicity, good will, conscience—beneath the conventional attitudes he has come abroad to represent are generosity and imagination. Later, little Bilham will say to him, "you're not a person to whom it's easy to tell things you don't want to know. Though it *is* easy, I admit—it's quite beautiful . . . when you do want to." When Maria first asks Strether what, if he should fail, he stands to lose, he exclaims. "Nothing!" As she leaves him, she asks once more, "What do you stand to lose?"

> Why the question now affected him as other he couldn't have said; he could only this time meet it otherwise. "Everything."

Has he come at last to reject the old language-game he has brought from Woollett, to reverse the meanings of "succeed" and "fail"? Later, in Paris with his dogged fellow American Waymarsh, the question of when he will see Chad comes up.

> "Well," said Strether almost gaily, "I guess I don't know anything!" His gaiety might have been a tribute to the fact that the state he had been reduced to did for him again what had been done by his talk of the matter with Miss Gostrey at the London theatre. It was somehow enlarging.

The enlargement will take Strether to a vision of Chad and Mme de Vionnet, and of Paris itself, so large as to reverse all of his original judgments. When Strether learns that the "virtuous attachment" he has imagined is not what he thought, when he discovers that Mme de Vionnet is in fact Chad's mistress, he has come too far to revert to his earlier moral categories. He has already seen Mrs. Newsome's lack of imagination and force of will. He has not been able to budge her from her preconceptions, and all that is left is "morally and intellectually to get rid of her." He sees her "fine cold thought" as a "particularly large iceberg in a cool blue northern sea." And Maria complements his thought with her own: "There's nothing so magnificent—for making others feel you—as to have no imagination."

At Strether's final meeting with Mme de Vionnet in her apartment, the aristocratic setting promises support: the "things from far back—tyrannies of history, facts of type, values, as the painters said, of expression—all working for her and giving her the supreme chance, the chance . . . on a great occasion, to be natural and simple." Her lie and Chad's now seem to him "an inevitable tribute to good taste," even as he winces "at the amount of comedy involved" in his own misunderstanding. But what Strether learns is how helpless her passion for Chad has been. As she has put it obliquely, "The wretched self is always there, always making one somehow a fresh anxiety." And while she asserts that the "only safe thing is to give," she seems, after all, in her fear that Chad will leave her, "exploited." She has made Chad better; "but it came to our friend with supreme queerness that he was none the less only Chad." Strether finally exclaims to Mme de Vionnet, "You're afraid for your life!" Her aristocratic nature will not save her. Strether recalls the fate of Madame Roland, the "smell of revolution, the smell of the public temper—or perhaps simply, the smell of blood." He sees Mme de Vionnet at once as "the finest and subtlest creature" caught in a passion "mature, abysmal, pitiful."

After two reversals, then, Strether finds himself once more voicing a moral view. To Chad, who shows signs of being ready for Woollett and the "art" of advertising, who seems somewhat tired of Mme de Vionnet and perhaps unfaithful to her, Strether appeals "by all you hold sacred" to remain in Paris. Strether finally sees beneath the charm of his new manners Chad's limited consciousness; Chad has spoken of being tired of Mme de Vionnet "as he might have spoken of being tired of roast mutton for dinner." And Strether calls Chad to moral responsibility as intensely as he might once have done, but the moral vision comes now out of a breadth of consciousness that would have been unimaginable in his early talk with Maria Gostrey. "You owe her everything," he tells Chad, "very much more than she can ever owe you. You've in other words duties to her, of the most positive sort; and I don't see what other duties . . . can be held to go before them."

As Strether later recounts the meeting to Maria Gostrey, he recognizes the "portentous solemnity" of his moral view, but, he concludes, "I was made so." And he must leave Maria and Paris so as not to get anything for himself: "To be right." Just as the early moral attitudes had to give way to the more inclusive awareness that aesthetic ordering permitted, so now the scope of the aesthetic is in turn enlarged—but in a far different way and with much more at stake—by the concern with conduct. Mme de Vionnet is more and less than she was, Chad's change seems less complete, and even Maria and her "hundred cases and categories" must be surrendered to a final view that is sterner. "It was awkward, it was almost stupid, not to seem to prize" the beauty and knowledge in Maria's life and in her offer of love. But, as James put it in the "project" for the novel, Strether "has come so far through his little experience that he has come out on the other side—on the other side even of a union with Miss Gostrey. He must go back as he came—or rather, really, so quite other that, in comparison, marrying Miss Gostrey would be almost of the same order." The sternness comes of an acceptance of consciousness, with all its privileges and pains, at the expense of all else.

The Lone Exile:
James's *The Ambassadors* and *The American Scene*

Michael Seidel

"Pierced, Betimes, by the Sharp Outland Dart"

The transition from Laurence Sterne to Henry James is not as odd as it might seem. James, who in an early journey through France called himself a "sentimental traveller," writes of the visit to Paris by his fictional latecomer, Lambert Strether in *The Ambassadors*: "he has come so far through his total little experience that he has come out on the other side." The kind of experience of which James speaks, as I have argued [elsewhere] for Sterne's Parisian crossing, is rendered as much by the process of fiction as by its action; "the other side" is neither a complete narrative mystery nor a simple transcontinental romp, but an imaginative passage, a projection of the reality that supposedly inaugurates it. In that complex relation between novelistic mimesis—human events, activities, motives, manners, expressions, desires, fears—and the illusionistic space in which mimesis takes place, the notion of crossing to "the other side" literally perpetuates the metaphor that grants fiction its imaginative domain.

Late in *The Ambassadors* Maria Gostrey puts a question to Lambert Strether about his exilic crossing: " 'Where *is* your 'home' moreover now—what has become of it?' " In their next conversation she asks the question again and then answers it: " 'To what do you go home?' " Strether responds, " 'I don't know. There will always

---

From *Exile and the Narrative Imagination.* © 1986 by Yale University. Yale University Press, 1986.

be something.' 'To a great difference,' she said." Maria means difference not merely in terms of the situation that awaits Strether in America but in terms of what has penetrated and absorbed Strether's mind in Europe. Difference is a form of illusion that James constantly portrays in his fiction and in his autobiographical and travel writing. In *The Middle Years,* he writes of a return to Europe (in this instance to England).

> Not to be denied also, over and above this, is the downright pleasure of the illusion yet again created, the *apparent* transfer from the past to the present of the particular combination of things that did at its hour ever so directly operate and that isn't after all then drained of virtue, wholly wasted and lost, for sensation, for participation in the act of life, in the attesting sights, sounds, smells, the illusion, as I say, of the recording senses.

"Going again" provides a mimetic overlay to having gone before, just as returning to a difference becomes part of the experience of having left in the first place. In *The American Scene,* James speaks about what coming home means in terms of a different kind of illusion, a national romance.

> Nothing could be of a simpler and straighter logic: Europe had been romantic years before, because she was different from America; wherefore America would now be romantic because she was different from Europe. It was for this small syllogism then to meet, practically, the test of one's repatriation; and as the palpitating pilgrim disembarked, in truth, he had felt it, like the rifle of a keen sportsman, carried across his shoulder and ready of instant use.

If exile enchants the ground of native territory, refamiliarization always writes its new romance. James is a pilgrim again—he does the land's history over. His return is an opportunity to confront territory made new and wild for its reinscription, something that seems to happen for James whenever Americans are on the move, going or coming. He even writes of the Europeanization of the American as "one's having been so pierced, betimes, by the sharp outland dart as to be able ever afterwards but to move about, vaguely and helplessly, with the shaft still in one's side" (*American Scene*). In the preface to *The Ambassadors,* James sets up the scene of Strether's Parisian adventure with a similar image: "the *situation* clearly would spring from the play of wildness and the development of extremes." To approach territory anew as a rifled pilgrim, or bedarted exile, and seek from it deliverance is, in a way, to make it originary, whether upon the virgin shores of America or in the refined historical spaces of Paris. Of Strether's outland European mission, James writes that he was "launched in something of which the sense would be quite disconnected from the sense of his past and which was literally beginning there and then."

In *The Ambassadors*, Lambert Strether goes to a Europe he had known just over a quarter century before; in *The American Scene*, James returns to an America after just under a quarter-century absence. Of his own exile from home James wrote that he considered himself a native of two continents and an outcast from both: "I saw, moreover, that I should be an eternal outsider." At the same time, to move in any direction is to experience something of a homecoming. He writes of the beginning of his quarter-century European exile that by returning to the Paris of his youth he was "restored to air already breathed and to a harmony already disclosed." To be in Paris for James is to increase the range of his sensations, to add to the present that exilic supplement he always carries, that "whole perfect Parisianism I seemed to myself always to have possessed mentally," a prospect not so different in its effect, though different in its timing, from that of Strether's in *The Ambassadors*.

To read *The Ambassadors* next to *The American Scene* is to get a special insight into the mind of the novelist, equal in many ways to the insights produced by the prefaces James provided for the novels themselves. *The American Scene* is the product of an admitted exilic consciousness—*Return of the Native* is the title James would have chosen had not Hardy already appropriated it. James's American return invites its own visionary record: "I was to return with much of the freshness of eye, outward and inward, which, with the further contribution of a state of desire, is commonly held a precious agent of perception." The impulse is the same in the preface to *The Ambassadors* when James writes of Strether's experience in Paris: "The answer to which is that he now at all events *sees;* so that the business of my tale and the march of my action, not to say the precious moral of everything, is just my demonstration of this process of vision."

"Seeing" in *The American Scene,* as it does in all James's fiction, combines vision as the mimetic record of places, events, people, institutions, manners, and vision as the aesthetic record of formal comprehension extending beyond the mere incremental march or succession of things sighted. James claims he is "fresh" as an "inquiring stranger," and not so disoriented as to cease to see as an "initiated native." His exilic bias grants him the privilege of fresh enchantments within familiar boundaries, grants him, that is, those special visionary coordinates on imaginatively primed ground. What is most intriguing about the way James "sees" in *The American Scene* is that his vision is comparative and double. For example, upon his return back to the East after he has been in the Far West, James reimposes the very kinds of distinctions he makes in his novels between America and Europe, just as he will later transpose similar distinctions to the temporal relation between the New North and the Old South. Coming back into New York State, James writes of

> the absurdest sense of meeting again a ripe old civilization and travelling through a country that showed the mark of established manners. It will seem, I fear, one's perpetual refrain, but the moral was yet once more that values of a certain order are, in such conditions, all relative, and that, as some wants of the spirits *must* somehow be met, one knocks together any substitute that will fairly stay the appetite.

The substitute supplies for the imagination what is wanted; James in this instance is not so much describing actual phenomena as creating those which he can then "see." When he does go south in *The American Scene,* he makes another substitution that has already appeared, under comparable imaginative circumstances, in *The Ambassadors.*

> On the one hand nothing could "say" more to the subject long expatriated, condemned by the terms of his exile to a chronic consciousness of grey northern seas, than to feel how, from New York, or even from Boston, he had but to sit still in his portentous car [to become aware of] the gradual soft, the distinctively demoralized, conversion of the soul of Nature. This conversion, if I may so put it without profanity, has always struck me, on any south-ward course, as a return, on the part of that soul, from a comparatively grim Theistic faith to the ineradicable prin-

ciple of Paganism; a conscious casting-off of the dread of theological abstraction—an abstraction still, even with all Puritan stiffening—in the interest of multiplied, lurking, familiar powers; divinities, graces, presences as unseen but as inherent as the scents clinging to the folds of Nature's robe.

This passage, of course, recalls the moment in *The Ambassadors* when Strether senses something "Pagan" in the young man, Chad Newsome, transposed from a gray, stern, material New England to a relaxed, bright, sensual Paris: "What could there be in this for Strether but the hint of some self-respect, some sense of power, oddly perverted; something latent and beyond access, ominous and perhaps enviable? The intimation had the next thing, in a flash, taken on a name—a name on which our friend seized as he asked himself if he weren't perhaps really dealing with an irreducible young Pagan." But there is in the move south for James in *The American Scene* something else that touches on the supplementary power of places in his fiction. As he moves even farther south through the Carolinas toward Florida, James writes: "Every breath that one might still have drawn in the South—might if twenty other matters had been different—haunted me as the thought of a lost treasure." The difference, of course, is the residue of slavery and the Civil War, but the airwaves of impressions James receives are like the impressions of an older Europe for James and for so many of his characters, impressions of history, of care, of texture, of scale. And the phrase, "a lost treasure," is one of those aesthetically material images that haunts James's imaginative sensibility from the artifacts of the *Spoils of Poynton* to the jewel of Paris in *The Ambassadors* to the eponymous *Golden Bowl*.

POWERS PLENIPOTENTIARY

Exilic action, as Maria Gostrey implies, is the illusion, and perhaps even the pathos, of a "great difference." In this sense, the action of *The Ambassadors* portrays what James calls a disparity so complete between New England America and France as that "between a life led in trees, say, and a life led in sea depths, or in other words between that of climbers and swimmers—or (crudely) that of monkeys and fish." James works the very notion of difference into the generic constituencies of the novel's plot. Consider the following narrative action:

A new and aggrandizing culture to the west fulminates after one of its glorious products has been lured to a refined and ancient civilization somewhat to the east, whose energies reside more in present intensities than promised futurities. The action focuses on the last stages of an ongoing struggle, a stalemate almost, between the impatience of the newer culture and the wiles of the older. In a burst of energy the forces from the emergent culture resolve to retrieve their abducted prize even after it appears that the supposed victim has been transformed into a half-willing captive. The older civilization puts up a game display of its virtues before ultimately relinquishing both its abductee and its cause, though the precise moment of relinquishment has not yet arrived when the present action ceases.

In the midst of the retrieval mission, the chief proponent for the emergent western culture undergoes a severe crisis of conscience, entertaining grave doubts about the values embodied, indeed, that he himself embodies, in perpetuating the cause of the forces that have marshaled him for the repatriation of its absconded human "property." Doubts concerning what might be called the grounds of the action become literal when the marshal for retrieval actually sets up dilatory residence in the alien land, shifting allegiance from the dominant will of the homefront to the ethos of the supposed antagonist culture. The original mission is, in a sense, fulfilled, but only at considerable cost to its participants, especially the waivering hero, who, toward the end of the action, seems no longer motivated by events as they occur sequentially, but experiences things, as it were, under revision, as if life has moved beyond that realm where destiny follows choice.

One more detail: the supposed victim from the west has been ensnared, and, in a way, captivated, by Paris.

Obviously, this narrative paradigm or mythos "belongs" to *The Ambassadors*. But in narrative legend Paris is as much a person as a place, and there is nothing in the sequence I have described that does not conform point for point to a plot as old as the dusty hills of Mycenae and the undulating plains of the Troas, the abduction of Helen by Paris that sets off the action of the Homeric *Iliad*. The renegade victim from the emergent West is male in James's case, Chad Newsome of Woollett, Massachusetts. Chad, whose epithet for himself at one point is "the lone exile," finds that he has been made over by Paris just as Helen of Troy, loved by Paris, temporarily gives up the role of Spartan *hausfrau* to take on, as femme fatale, the name of the rival city and culture that most elegantly displays her. Both exiles become, in a sense, voluntary; they cross to a zone of opportunity that readily serves as a metaphoric space for the state of their altered consciousnesses.

The idea of the transforming space is an enduring one in imaginative literature, especially if attendant upon its occupation is the cultural rupture that occurs when different civilizations or societies seem to want to "time" things in different ways, when marvelous but spent civilizations try to give pause to the orders that will efface them. For James, Paris is the same lure and threat to the ethos of America that Troy was for the Greeks. Paris is otherness, and for those who do not have it in their blood or being to acclimatize to it, it is even further "other" than its location in the west of Europe. The tricks of metaphoric analogy and the transports of epic memory project James's scene farther east and farther back into a forbidden and lustful past. Paris is "the vast bright Babylon" that sustains the notion of the overrefined, alluring place where the material, enterprising world can be, at least, well lost.

As the brightest jewel of Catholic Europe, Paris evokes in its Babylonian image the traditional Protestant horror of the city as Church, the old temptress herself, the Whore of Babylon; and when James begins the second half of his novel, the program for European salvation, in the very confines of Notre Dame Cathedral, the scene calls up a passage from the earlier sequence in the old feudal city of Chester: "The Catholic Church for Waymarsh—that was to say the enemy, the monster of bulging eyes and far-reaching quivering groping tentacles—was exactly society, exactly the multiplication of shibboleths, exactly the discrimination of types and tones, exactly the wicked old Rows of Chester, rank with feudalism; exactly in short Europe."

Strether, through the course of the novel, finds himself estranged from Waymarsh and the new American mission when he discovers himself on Paris's side. There is something there "more acute in manners, more sinister in morals, more fierce in the national life," and he later finds himself, he was "amused to think, on the side of the fierce, the sinister, the acute." The best place for him in Paris is, indeed, the apartment of its most alluring temptress, Madame de Vionnet, who seems to have just the right collection of things to reflect a lost epic order that made up a "vista, which he found high melancholy and sweet—full, once more, of dim historic shades, of the faint far-away cannon-roar of the great Empire." As James writes of Strether in his "Project" for *The Ambassadors*, Madame de Vionnet "gratifies some more distinctively disinterested aesthetic, intellectual, social, even, so to speak, historic sense in him." Her Paris for Strether is, in a certain sense, comparable to what James in *The American Scene* calls "the epic age" of the Old South, beset, if not by Baron von Haussmann's city planners, then by northern carpetbaggers who pillage a land, after its four epic years, "disinherited of art or of letters."

In his eulogy for James, Ezra Pound recognized the epic, national proportions of many of the novels: "In his books he showed race against race, immutable; the essential Americanness, or Englishness or Frenchness—in *The American,* the difference between one nation and another; not flag-waving and treaties, not the machinery of government, but 'why' there is always misunderstanding, why men of different race are not the same" (*Literary Essays of Ezra Pound*). Though in *The Ambassadors* James sets his novel's epic proportions deliberately and arranges them with considerable force, the result is not an array of structural parallels in the manner, say, of Joyce's absorption of the Homeric *Odyssey* into *Ulysses* but a model for action that conforms to the comparison James draws himself to *Antony and Cleopatra,* a play that with a few adjustments mirrors the identical exilic plot: Egypt is to Rome what Troy is to Greece what Europe is to America.

The larger casus belli of such a plot always stems from the alienation of native affection and the rage that alienation inspires. Strether and his friend Waymarsh starkly frame the situation for *The Ambassadors* in reference to Chad's fellow exile, the young American little Bilham: " 'Why don't he go home?' " asks Waymarsh. " 'Well, because he likes it over here,' " answers Strether. A similar question might be asked and a similar answer rendered for Helen of Sparta and

Antony of Rome, be they in Troy or Alexandria: " 'Why don't they go home?' 'Well, because they like it over here.' "

There is, of course, more to what Richard Blackmur, in a nice phrase, calls the "sensitized deep form" of *The Ambassadors* than the rudiments of its international epic plotting. As James wrote of his novel to Hugh Walpole, "it *is* probably a very *packed* production, with a good deal of one thing within another." Much has been written about these "things," about James's refinement of novelistic language, about his scenic richness, about his conversant intellect, about his portrayal of well-imagined and imagining beings. But even if for the moment we limit matters to the realm of plot, *The Ambassadors* comes more firmly packed than I have so far suggested. For example, James enfolds another classically derived action within the exilic adventure. Consider the following:

> A family scion prompted by desires of an initiatory nature, predominantly sexual, finds himself in conflict with obligations that are of a familial and financial nature. He strives to achieve a balance between promptings and obligations that will allow him his moment in the sun, his prime time, before resumption of conventional responsibilities. During the interval of readjustment, an older male delegate, materially aligned with the family interests, finds himself exposed to a world of charged sensibilities. He moves from the brink of male menopause to the brink of sexual infatuation. Forces from and of the family seek to rescue both scion and *senex* advisor from the lure of prompting enticements. Both rescuers and enticers gauge the best strategic means to negotiate and compromise so that most may be gained or least be lost. Actors and actresses in this scenario act or do not act in relation to benefits that in one way or another accrue to their credit or discredit in both a material and ethical sense.

I have described, very roughly, a pattern of action generally applicable to *The Ambassadors* that is also a standard variant of comic plotting available from Greek new comedy to contemporary jet set farce. Chad Newsome is the young, wayward scion; Lambert Strether a "belated" *senex* adventurer and convert. The intricate and calculated way James combines his comic and epic plots is one of the glories of *The Ambassadors*. The diagram below outlines the relation of the parts to the generic whole.

COMIC MISSION

BOOK 1: American Dispensation: Mrs. Newsome of Woollett; Strether's arrival in Europe as agent for Chad's return.

BOOK 2: Arrival of primary Ambassador (Strether) on Parisian scene.

BOOK 3: Strether and surrogate American: little Bilham in Chad's apartment.

BOOK 4: Crucial negotiation with Chad for his American return.

BOOK 5: Gloriani's garden epiphany (first "super-sensual hour").

BOOK 6: Strether's first promise to Madame de Vionnet ("I'll save you if I can").

EPIC SALVATION

BOOK 7: European Dispensation: Notre Dame of Paris; Strether as agent for postponement of Chad's return.

BOOK 8: Arrival of secondary Ambassador (Sarah Pocock) on Parisian scene.

BOOK 9: Strether and surrogate American: Mamie Pocock in Sarah's hotel.

BOOK 10: Crucial negotiation with Sarah for Chad's remaining in Europe.

BOOK 11: Rural seat epiphany (second "super-sensual hour").

BOOK 12: Strether's second promise to Madame de Vionnet that he will ask Chad "never to forsake her."

A legitimate question to ask of James's venturings into epic and comic plots is what appeal would such schemes have for him? And part of an answer involves his understanding of what might be called the concentric pressures operating on individual characters in distinction to the eccentric appeal of the exilic or international imagination. But these pressures and appeals are difficult to separate, and James's adaptation of traditional plots, melding nationally and socially determined obligations with the finer tuning of individual consciousnesses, gives his work real dimension. T. S. Eliot remarked that James's characters are constituents of a greater social entity, which can be more or less true of any fiction but which is surely true of action on the scale James presents it. Thus the intensely personal and complex drive to absorb qualities one lacks or discard qualities one abhors is often frustrated by defenses and loyalties that one carries as part of a national baggage. It is as Ralph Touchett says in *Portrait of a Lady:* "Ah, one doesn't give up one's country any more than one gives up one's grandmother. They're both antecedent to choice, elements of one's composition that are not to be eliminated."

CROSS-PURPOSES

Initially, Strether has two jobs to do in America's cause, neither of which is very subtle but both of which are empowered by his porfolio as Ambassador from Woollett. Strether is reminded of his national burden when he sees his friend Waymarsh, a Connecticut Yankee in the west of Queen Victoria's realm. Strether, "for his part, felt once more like Woollett in person." His first job is to present the details of his mission to Chad, the business proposition that Mrs. Newsome offers her son in regard to taking on the advertising department of the home enterprise, what James, emphasizing his version of progressive America, calls in the "Project" for the novel "the bustling business at home, the mercantile mandate, the counter, the ledger, the bank, the 'advertising interest,' [all of which] embody mainly the special phase of civilization to which he must recall his charge." Strether's second job is not to have his first fail to take effect; that is, he must not only inform Chad but reform his exilic propensities, return him to the native material fold. The payoff for Strether is Mrs. Newsome's hand in marriage.

Strether's American mission, the ostensible purpose for his crossing, is tied to the letter of economic and familial law, but it was only after he performed its first part, laying the ledger on the table, that he began to realize that the second part of his mission, making it work, had much less to do with the possibility of his failing Mrs. Newsome at home than with betraying his new international self. The fact that Strether considered himself "a perfectly equipped failure" in America is precisely what Mrs. Newsome counted on to ensure against his failing her in Europe. But ambassadors exist so that they might make compromises, and the question for Strether is what kind of compromises he has already made and what kind he can afford to keep making.

Strether begins with good intentions toward his American mission. He wishes to get matters over with quickly, virtually blurting out his demands—a middle-aged "now see here!"—to a polite Chad. James calls Strether's quick pitch a "night-attack," which is efficient but not very ceremonious. Later, Strether's much vaguer but more compelling commitment to save Madame de Vionnet requires, if nothing else, time to contemplate options. The buying of time against the enterprise of repatriation is represented in the figuration E. M. Forster projected as the novel's hourglass pattern, and the figure is wonderfully descriptive of action as temporal purchase. Strether no longer serves as the material agent for a family factory, but as a barterer for Europe's historical, epochal, and epic time, the slow, steady accretions of what culture needs to save itself. It is in this sense that the quality of the European experience alters everything for him, makes him imaginatively exilic. His situation in Paris is not altogether different, at least structurally, from the prototypical temporizing epic *salvator,* Achilles, whose refusal to act on behalf of the aggrieved home forces in the *Iliad* seems vaguely echoed in *The Ambassadors* when Strether says of himself " 'the hero has taken refuge in his corner. He's scared at his heroism—he shrinks from his part.' " Wronged families always want action; individual conscience takes time. Achilles sulks and makes of his tent a little Troy; Strether stalls and forces the home front to dispatch a second wave of ambassadors joined by Waymarsh as a kind of Agamemnon.

Strether's subtle shift in allegiances when "exposed to the action of another air" is his special fate—it singles him out like Achilles, like Antony, as he will learn when the second, more loyal, more national ambassadorial mission, headed by the matriarchal surrogate, Sarah Pocock, arrives to consider whether it is even worthwhile to bother retrieving *him.* Some Americans, like Waymarsh, are homeward bound in whatever direction they move; others are more comfortably exposed to "another air." In the conflict of cultural values that makes up the implicit action of the novel, Maria Gostrey acts to repatriate Americans who deserve it and to provide a European itinerary for those who have the capacity to appreciate the "outland"; she is an agent of the border police against interlopers: "I'm—with all my

The Ambassadors and The American Scene / 135

other functions—an agent for repatriation. I want to re-people our stricken country. What will become of it else? I want to discourage others."

Strether, even at the beginning of his European experience, is intrigued by what he calls, picking up a mock-epic cadence, "the enemy's country." In a conversation with Maria, he begins to doubt what it means to be a "good American." He complains before he knows what he intends: " 'Oh hang it,' " and we hear immediately: "It represented, this mute ejaculation, a final impulse to burn his ships. These ships, to the historic muse, may seem of course mere cockles, but when he presently spoke to Miss Gostrey it was with the sense at least of applying the torch. 'Is it then a conspiracy?' " If so, it is a conspiracy at the expense of America, balanced cleverly by James in the comic plot when Waymarsh conspires with America against an increasingly Europeanized Strether. As Strether moves through Europe by moving from Maria Gostrey to Madame de Vionnet, his friend Waymarsh gets re-Americanized by deserting Miss Barrace for the new American ambassador, Sarah Pocock. Exile is a chiasmus or narrative crossing.

It is precisely when the other or "alien" race gets under Strether's distinctly American skin in *The Ambassadors* that the complex and imaginatively textured European experience has the effect of reducing his perceived social, indeed, racial obligations to America and to the values James sees as nationally disposed. On the other hand, James, by his own testimony in the preface to his eponymously titled *The American,* embarked on an enterprise in which he realized that his fiction still staked its American claim in the very teeth of its greater European resource. James's dilemma was equivalent in some ways to that of Maria Gostrey as go-between in *The Ambassadors* when she says: " 'I bear on my back the huge load of our national consciousness, or, in other words—for it comes to that—of our nation itself.' "

Since consciousness is actionable in James's fiction, it is clear that James's American load, like Maria's, is one that he might be tempted, at any given time, to jettison, but could not, for various reasons, manage to do. Many of his characters, including Strether, operate under the same strain. James makes this clear early and late in *The Ambassadors.* He writes in the preface that the most notable thing about Strether is his nationality: "Possessed of our friend's nationality, to start with, there was a general probability in his narrower localism; which, for that matter, one had really but to keep under the lens for an hour to see it give up its secrets." Strether's nature and his localism bespeak New England denial, which makes for a natural conflict when the sexual juices of the plot begin to flow and the resonances of the international theme begin to sound. When Maria Gostrey senses that in his walk with her he is indulging in something he does not think right, Strether concludes that he must be displaying enjoyment. She describes his reluctance to enjoy himself as his failure; he attributes it to " 'the failure of Woollett. *That's* general.' " Though he is capable of joking about it, Strether still takes a kind of pride in his localism even later in the novel. It is not so much his American citizenship he gives up as the credentials for the particular ambassadorial mission upon which he was "launched." He says to little Bilham in regard to his admiration for Mamie Pocock: " 'I've been sacrificing so to strange gods that I feel I want to put on record, somehow, my fidelity—fundamentally unchanged after all—to our own.' "

This tension that marks the design of the novel, its local obligations and international longings, seems confirmed with Strether's first understanding of Chad's Parisian liaison, an understanding not as mistaken as his second concerning its virtuousness: "Was there in Chad, by chance, after all, deep down, a principle of aboriginal loyalty that had made him, for sentimental ends, attach himself to elements, happily encountered, that would remind him most of the old air and the old soil?" There is an interplay of phrasings in *The Ambassadors* that identifies American contingents whatever Europeanized values they might imbibe. At one point while Strether is struggling over the issue of just exactly what happens to the American consciousness saturated in the splendors of Europe, Maria Gostrey says of the most dandified of the Americans, little Bilham, the very object of Strether's plea in Gloriani's garden for that Pagan intensity presumably missing in America, " 'Oh he's all right. He's one of *us!*' " meaning that he, like them, is an American, pierced by the outland dart, but, also, that he, like them, is simply American. Later, Chad uses the same phrase of himself, " 'Oh I'm all right!' " to suggest that he has lost the sense of neither his origins nor his obligations. In *The American Scene,* when James worries about the character of America and the state of its progressivism, he hears the voice of the Demos, the spirit that makes the people and the land "different" in ways that Europe will never know. America is an "enormous family of rugged, of almost ragged, rustics—a tribe of sons and daughters too numerous to be counted and homogeneous perhaps to monotony." James's own response picks up the very idiom of the place: "Oh, the *land's* all right!" Americans can never go entirely wrong because they are vague about their deficiencies. The surface their imaginations rarely penetrate is an amiable one; the despondency of cultural paralysis is "foreign" to them. Chad in his person makes this argument for *The Ambassadors,* and what James says in *The American Scene* about the amiability of the American rich applies to the young Mr. Newsome: "The amiability proceeds from an essential vagueness; whereas real haughtiness is never vague about itself—it is only vague about others."

MATRIARCHY AND THE WASH OF GOLD

It is of great importance to *The Ambassadors* that so much of its represented action is controlled by an unrepresented figure, Mrs. Newsome, who sits invisibly powerful at home, judging, in a sense, all that goes on abroad. Strether begins, as he later notes of Jim Pocock, by serving "essentially a society of women"; he takes his marching orders, as Maria Gostrey puts it, in such a way as to receive " 'at the point of the bayonet a whole moral and intellectual being or block.' " When he lingers too long in Europe, supposedly in the swim with Madame de Vionnet, whose commerce with Strether, negotiated almost spiritually from the Cathedral of Notre Dame, seems to Sarah Pocock "hideous," Sarah asks, " 'what is your conduct but an outrage to women like *us?*' "

The sets of differences that mark Americans and Europeans are located, for the most part, in images of women, who, like the controlling deities of the *Iliad,* are influential, determinate, and national. If the *Iliad* has its stern, unattached Athena behind the Greek cause and the wife-goddess Hera behind the Trojan, *The Ambassadors* boasts of Mrs. Newsome, the ever-absent, ever-present doyenne of the American factory, and, on the Continental side, Marie de Vionnet, with the image of the Catholic Mary, Notre Dame, in the background. Strether's switch in allegiances from the "moral swell" of Woollett to the "pathos" of Madame de Vionnet determines the fate of his consciousness: "It marked for himself the flight of time, or at any rate what he was pleased to think of with irony and pity as the rush of experience; it having been but the day before yesterday that he sat at her feet and held on by her garment and was fed by her hand. It was the proportions that were changed, and the proportions were at all times, he philosophised, the very conditions of perception, the terms of thought." National and social proportions turn to aesthetic ones, the projection or the "performance of 'Europe.' " Utility gives way to intensity. Actresses such as Madame de Vionnet play Cleopatra or, more affecting yet, the deserted Dido of the *Aeneid.*

In Europe, as Chad's experience and, subsequently, Strether's bear out, women tend not to negotiate from positions of familial power but to persuade as the transmitters, the molders of behavior that is "wonderful," as Miss Barrace keeps putting it, that is culturally and perhaps even sexually awesome. In *The American Scene,* James distinguishes between the American and the European woman: "she had been grown in an air in which a hundred of the 'European' complications and dangers didn't exist." The American woman is, for James, the very symbol of utility in an aggrandizing social economy. In *The Ambassadors*, Waymarsh says of Mamie Pocock, " 'her full beauty is only for those who know how to make use of her,' " and in *The American Scene* James says of the American woman: "It has been found among them that, for more reasons than we can now go into, her manner of embodying and representing her sex has fairly made of her a new human convenience, not unlike fifty of the others, of a slightly different order, the ingenious mechanical appliances, stoves, refrigerators, sewing-machines, type-writers, cash-registers, that have done so much, in the household and the place of business, for the American name." When Strether refuses to identify the utilitarian item of Woollett manufacture in *The Ambassadors* marketed by the factory presently controlled by the will, if not the effort, of Mrs. Newsome, it may be because he doesn't have to. The item is the "new convenience" of American matriarchy.

In the larger view of the action, Strether's delay in rescuing Chad Newsome becomes a political or ideological affront, an assault on the matriarchal home front. And the politics might even be conceived as internecine even if, and when, the absconded American heir returns home and struggles with his sister for the future. As Chad says of Sarah's probable motives, she wants him in her own American sphere because " 'when you hate you want to triumph, and if she should get me neatly stuck there she *would* triumph.' "

American battles are fought in different ways and on different turf than exilic ones in a European theater.

Chad's European performance, and soon Strether's, are anathema to the new set of American representatives in France, led by the family's vice-regent, Sarah Pocock, who seems to prefer events like the circus to the theatrical or salon life of Paris. Hers is the arena of the Demos. When James analyzed the features of the American family in *The American Scene,* he sensed a certain arriviste quality: "family life is in fact, as from child to parent, from sister to brother, from wife to husband, from employed to employer, the eminent field of the democratic demonstration." For James the "active Family" is "a final social fact," the People, he calls them, who enjoy every easy convenience of being American.

> That's their interest—that they *are* the people; for what interest, under the sun, would they have if they weren't? They are the people "arrived," and, what is more, disembarked: that's all the difference. It seems a difference because elsewhere (in "Europe," say again), though we see them begin, at the very most, to arrive, socially, we yet practically see them still on the ship—we have never yet seen them disembark thus *en masse.*

It is almost as if James in this passage from a book describing his return home to America remembered the American arriviste family of *The Ambassadors* depositing itself on the shores of an older, refined European civilization.

Family democracy, the source of the comic enterprise in *The Ambassadors,* runs completely counter to the image of the imperial European lure who so intrigues first Chad and then Strether in the figure of Madame de Vionnet. Marie's effort is, finally, anti-American; she seeks to hold for the present what has been her past. About the future she is almost inarticulate. One of James's complaints against the newness of America in *The American Scene* is the land's perpetual repudiation of the past, "so far as there had been a past to repudiate." James's distrust of the speed of American production plays upon a different sense of "production," an imaginative and aesthetic one: "There we catch the golden truth which so much of the American world strikes us as positively organized to gainsay, the truth that production takes time, and that the production of interest, in particular, takes *most* time."

In *The American Scene,* time is money, and it cannot buy European experience: "expensive as we are, we have nothing to do with continuity, responsibility, transmission, and don't in the least care about what becomes of us after we have served our present purpose." James does not condemn the existence of money so much as wonder at what it purchases—what connection expense has to value as the basis for America's "accommodation of life."

> This basis is that of active pecuniary gain and of active pecuniary gain only—that of one's making the conditions so triumphantly pay that the prices, the manners, the other inconveniences, take their place as a friction it is comparatively easy to salve, wounds directly treatable with the wash of gold. What prevails, what sets the tune, is the American scale of gain, more magnificent than any other, and the fact that the whole assumption, the whole theory of life, is that of the individual's participation in it, that of his being more or less punctually and more or less effectually "squared." To make so much money that you won't, that you don't "mind," don't mind anything—that is absolutely, I think, the main American formula.

The best trick in James's anti-Gilded Age rhetoric here is the set of quotation marks around "mind," as if the lack of caring is also the lack of thinking, a notion perhaps behind Strether's wish at the beginning of *The Ambassadors* that his old friend Waymarsh, "the exile from Milrose," would not be the first "note" of Europe for him. Waymarsh, who goes through Europe on the forward incline, sees his exilic experience as a conspiracy to keep him away from newspapers, "an elaborate engine for dissociating the confined American from that indispensable knowledge," which rendered him his sense of an established order. Progressive, future-rendering America needs "new" information; it does not thrive on what constitutes tradition. The real old Europe belongs to that lost historical sense that Madame de Vionnet represents for Strether—a Europe of refinement and almost forlorn vestigiality. In Paris he feels "odd starts of the historic sense, suppositions and divinations with no warrant but their intensity."

When Strether first arrives in Europe he is still enmeshed in a system of values that turns on money. He cannot quite understand what Maria Gostrey means when she says that she doesn't "do"

Europe with American travelers for money but for national necessity. Bewildered, Strether responds: " 'You can scarcely be said to
do it for love.' He waited a moment. 'How do we reward you?' "
" 'You don't!' " returns Maria. It is as if Strether has not yet seen
that the European venture will involve something other than cash
flow, that it will involve the separation of his pleasure from the
financial and social ordinance that supports it. In a telling Jamesian
figure that reinforces the impending abandonment of the American
mission, Strether seems glad at the prospect of some free time in
England before encountering Waymarsh: "he was like a man who,
elatedly finding in his pocket more money than usual, handles it a
while and idly and pleasantly chinks it before addressing himself to
the business of spending." Paradoxically, the more he spends toward
"change," the less he will rely on his substantial American line of
credit. Indeed, Strether uses the phrase "disinherited beyond appeal"
for the latter stages of his deteriorating relations with Mrs. Newsome.

When Strether stops hearing from Mrs. Newsome entirely, he
loses his credit but gains validity, a more imaginative resource. This
makes an earlier discussion between Strether and Maria Gostrey of
great interest. Strether says of Mrs. Newsome that she is high-
strung, nervous. Maria puts it epigrammatically: " 'You mean she's
an American invalid?' " Strether says he would not put it quite that
way, but she is American to the core and would consent to being, in
a sense, *invalid,* to remain an American. The substance of what
happens in the novel turns on Strether's invalidation of the material
mission in order to appreciate, in all senses of the word, the
European supplement. He faces with equanimity what Chad calls the
sharpest of sharp facts about his predicament: " 'you give up money.
Possibly a good deal of money.' " To do so is to give up, as exile,
one version of America.

Meanwhile, Chad, whom Strether on Marie's behalf begs to
remain in Europe, takes up on his own behalf the American material
obligation. As little Bilham puts it, Chad "has his possible future
before him." Sooner or later he will terminate his exilic adventure
and go home. His language reveals the direction in which he points:
" 'But I'm coming around—I'm not so bad now.' " Chad comes
around to America and to an American idiom; he uses "bad" as his
sister might use it, as the uxorious Jim Pocock might use it, as the
American Family entire might use it in relation to Europe. To be able

to use the word that way is to have made the American circuit. And Strether does not reamin oblivious to the turning force of egoism in Chad, the certainty that no matter what else happens he will act as is best for him, which is to say best for him as an American. James can be devastating on Chad when the mood strikes him, and his language picks up the metaphor of turnarounds that so marks the action and the novel's plot: "Chad was always letting people have their way when he felt that it would somehow turn his wheel for him."

COMING OUT

Chad's readiness at the end of *The Ambassadors* to leave the place that initiated him may resolve the conventional comic plot of the novel but leaves the international one in arrears. Strether much prefers his first impression of Chad, his first startling image of what might happen in the exilic place. Europe has made Chad anew, almost completely refashioned him, at least to Strether's eyes: "Chad had been made over. That was all; whatever it was it was everything. Strether had never seen the thing so done before—it was perhaps a speciality of Paris." This sort of initiatory scene has always been a part of Western civilization ever since the Renaissance invention of the grand tour. When James writes in *The Middle Years* of his own return to Paris in the 1870s he remembers what the original crossing meant to him, a memory that appears to partake of both Chad's and Strether's European experience, with its metaphors of sexual *tristesse* as well as "quickening" glory.

> To return at all across the years to the gates of the paradise of the first larger initiations is to be ever so tempted to pass them, to push in again and breathe the air of this, that and the other plot of rising ground particularly associated, for memory and gratitude, with the quickening process. The trouble is that with these sacred spots, to later appreciation, the garden of youth is apt inordinately to bristle, and that one's account of them has to shake them together fairly hard, making a coherent thing of them, to profit by the contribution of each.

The imaginative and sexual quickening is a process that Strether is slower than Chad or, for that matter, than James to register. This is so even after Strether attributes to Madame de Vionnet Chad's transformation in Paris: "he had created for himself a new set of circumstances." Little specific is either said or meant, partly because Strether avoids some of the obvious details, but what is always implied, in addition to the imposition of a smoother texture over a rougher native surface, is sexual familiarity. Maria Gostrey says of Chad that " 'two quite distinct things that—given the wonderful place he's in—may have happened to him. One is that he may have got brutalised. The other is that he may have got refined.' " What Maria really means to say is that *one* thing may have happened to Chad, but that one thing strikes particular viewers in *two* ways. It is when Strether begins to understand that the notion of brutalization is not really possible except to an aggrieved American mind that allegiances begin to shift. Brutalized could mean, in another context, libertinized or, as Strether says himself, "Paganized." He would have done well to have kept that possibility—even if differently conceived—in mind; it would have saved him some sexual surprises. Of refinement there could be no doubt in Chad's case, though even here James makes it clear—and Strether sees this only later—that Chad never abandons his rougher American egoism. He has merely learned to display himself with more skill during his Parisian hiatus. From a literal course in painting, he had graduated to what James calls "initiations more direct and more deep." Initiations are part of the exilic experience narrative creates and records.

What Strether sees in Chad, of course, is what James primes him to see as part of his own narrative adventure, a "transformation unsurpassed." Chad has experienced the "rupture of an identity," and what Strether says of him might be what he belatedly desires for himself and what generally takes place in the fictional invention of mimetic being: "You could deal with a man as himself—you couldn't deal with him as somebody else." The somebody else Strether envisages in Chad is a version of the somebody else Strether might have been. Strether later comes to realize that he has invested too much in Chad's newer consciousness without admitting its sexual implications for himself, a bad investment in that when Chad tries to assuage his accumulating guilt for readying to leave Marie, Strether has to assume the full debt with only a recent comprehension of its total nature.

One of the calculated ironies of *The Ambassadors* is that Chad tends to clear out of town just as Strether, in one way or another, moves in. This pattern occurs often enough in the novel to make one think that more than social spaces are negotiated; Chad seems to be giving everything over, including the image of the place and the woman who performs the initiating rites. Chad's American career promises a future in advertising, and his first advertising campaign is the selling of his options in Marie de Vionnet to Strether. Chad virtually offers her to Strether at their first introduction in Gloriani's garden, and when he leaves town toward the end of the novel, he does so to leave Strether alone with Marie, adding later an excuse about picking up "some news of the art of advertisement" in London. But, of course, Chad gives Strether only the "performance" of Madame de Vionnet; her person he keeps for himself. She is a European supplement that ought not place too severe a tax on Strether's developing imagination. Maria keeps warning Strether— she tells him that Chad is not free and assumes Strether knows what she's talking about. The same is true about little Bilham's famous description of the affair as a "virtuous attachment." Little Bilham means it is neither debilitating nor vulgar. Strether wishes it to mean *innocent,* which is precisely the word he uses later.

But this is to pick up Strether's own initiatory path somewhat down the road. If we look to his and Maria Gostrey's recollection of how Strether started, we can begin closer to the beginning and mark the initiation ceremony, both spatial and sexual, that still interests the two of them at the end of the novel, "the curiosity felt by both of them as to where he would 'come out.' They had so assumed it was to be in some wonderful place—they had thought of it as so very *much* out. Well, that was doubtless what it had been—since he had come out just there. He was out, in truth, as far as it was possible to be, and must now rather bethink himself of getting in again."

Strether begins his exilic progress as a "belated" adventurer, a trait he never quite loses: "he was for ever missing things through his general genius for missing them." Strether says of himself, " 'I don't get drunk; I don't pursue the ladies; I don't spend money; I don't even write sonnets. But nevertheless I'm making up late for what I didn't have early.' " He is always a little vague as to exactly what it is he is trying to make up: "what I want is a thing I've ceased to measure or even to understand." What he does do is register an almost continuous sense of difference and contrast: what he wants is what he lacks. Maria Gostrey senses as much immediately. She is more than Strether's "guide" to Europe, his Baedecker of civilized consciousness. She is also the pattern for a different kind of indulgence of the immediate, something that Strether never quite practices but comes around to expressing during the key scene in Gloriani's garden. Maria Gostrey is what Strether isn't; she has those "qualities and quantities that collectively figured to him as the advantage snatched from lucky chances."

Strether is an unlikely participant in the drama that is about to beset him, and if, as Miss Barrace says, he is supposed to perform in it as " 'the hero,' " he shrinks from the action that might make it momentous for him, sexual choice. In the "Project" for the novel, James says he did not want to represent every woman in the book to have "made up" to his hero, nor would he solve any narrative problem with a purely sexual choice in Strether's case, though he was not above complicating the narrative texture with sexual intrusions. James does admit, however, that he allows most of the women in the novel to appear agreeably affected by Strether. Strether does not seem all that grateful. When Madame de Vionnet says in public that all women love Strether, he assumes that "to say such things to a man in public, a woman must practically think of him as ninety years old." The fact is, despite his stirrings of new youth, that is the way he thinks of himself. There is, and could be, a large sexual component acted out in Strether's part, but James resists forcing his actor to act it. Strether prefers separating his imaginative ecstasies from his sexual latencies. The best he can do is feel his blood stir in the company of Parisian power. He equates place and fate as if something is bound to happen because Paris, especially old Paris, is the revolutionary arena with its "smell of revolution, the smell of the public temper—or perhaps simply the smell of blood." Strether's reference to the revolutionary Paris comports with his own rebellion from the clutches of Woollett, and the smell of blood, no matter how it flows, is for him the sign of vitality lacking in the "secret" repression of his New England "prison-house."

The strength of James's decision not to have Strether consciously traffic in sexual matters is tested by the opportunities the novel provides him with two women with variants of the same name, Maria and Marie. He militantly misses twice, even feeling uneasy at the challenge: "he had a horror, as he now thought of himself, of being in question between women." The irony of this situation mirrors part of the novel's chiastic structure: "it was others who looked abstemious and he who looked greedy; it was he somehow who finally paid, and it was others who mainly partook." It is not as if there are no full experiences for Strether in Paris, but he sees the fullest, Marie de Vionnet, more as an aesthetic and historical artifact than as the possessed Dido she appears at the end. Surely, Strether does not understand that for the likes of Dido or Helen of Troy or, indeed, Cleopatra, to whom he directly compares Marie, aesthetics and sexuality are indistinguishable.

Strether's reaction is not so much so proclaim the separation of aesthetic appreciation and physical desire as to ignore the intricacies of the combination. His reaction to any one piece of life's puzzle that confronts him in Europe during the few months of his mission is that it is too confusedly connected to the whole of the impression to make any distinct sense: " 'I can't separate—it's all one.' " Two things can be said about such a view. First, the experience is really imaginative and aesthetic and, as such, must be taken whole; and second, the experience is intensely sexual and any concentration on one of its parts would reveal the single piece of the puzzle upon which Strether resists focusing until it is forced upon him. Then he considers it a catastrophe. James as artist knows more than Strether admits as hero about the state of his frustration. In the "Project" for *The Ambassadors,* James carefully chooses a word that has both aesthetic and sexual connotations in reference to Strether: "disenchanted without having known any great enchantments, enchanters, or, above all, enchantresses." James recognizes that one basis of failure in life, as it was in his famous story, "The Beast in the Jungle," is missed sexual opportunity. Maria Gostrey asks a blunt question of Strether about Marie de Vionnet: " 'Are you really in love with her?' " Strether offers the bizarre answer: " 'It's of no importance I should know . . . It matters so little—has nothing to do, practically, with either of us.' " But, to be fair to Strether, James is not entirely certain how gained sexual opportunity transfers from private circumstance to the integrity of the imagination.

PARISIAN SUPPLEMENTS

Strether's resistance to what James in all his international novels advertises as a key ingredient of the exilic adventure leads to an initiatory scene that is itself belated in *The Ambassadors,* coming as it does so near the end of the action, the scene of the rural retreat when

Strether witnesses evidence of the liaison whose likelihood he had so long denied. Ironically, his own intimacies with Madame de Vionnet made others think he was "as much in the swim [with her] as anybody else," and long before the country scene, Strether says of Madame de Vionnet that "she thus publicly drew him into her boat." He uses the metaphor as an analogue for his passionate interest in her case—though even he is not exactly sure where the passion lies—but his language also suggests a switch from his transatlantic mission to an inland waterway: "He took up an oar and, since he was to have the credit of pulling, pulled." The credit he loses after wasting the price of Mrs. Newsome's steamship ticket he assumes from Madame de Vionnet's rowboat. Sarah and Waymarsh naturally see him as "launched in a relation," though Strether protests that he "had never really been launched at all." The metaphor builds to its finest irony in the rural scene when Strether discovers for certain that the sexual relationship between Chad and Marie de Vionnet is neither virtuous in his sense of it nor innocent in anyone's. He discovers the lovers rowing in a small boat, or, to put it another way, he discovers how embarrassing it is to think one's self in someone's boat when another already occupies the only vacant seat.

Strether's own reverie-like metaphor for the day of the country retreat places him in the midst of a landscape painting that he remembers he would have liked to purchase. And the image of the small boat coming around the bend in the river provides a double shock; Chad was not only sitting in the boat Strether had already appropriated metaphorically, but he was also in the picture of the day Strether had just worked so hard to draw up. Before the country discovery, Strether had refused to talk about Chad on the last two occasions of visiting Marie de Vionnet. This, he said, gave him the sense with her of "fulness and frequency." Clearly, Chad had been, in a symbolic way, sexually displaced, even if Strether was unaware of it.

Before his awakening Strether describes the scene as a pastoral idyll: "a land of fancy for him—the background of fiction, the medium of art, the nursery of letters; practically as distant as Greece, but practically also well-nigh as consecrated. Romance could weave itself, for Strether's sense, out of elements mild enough." When sex enters this rural seat, it does so like the figure of Death in Arcadia, "a marked drop into innocent friendly Bohemia." Strether's explanation for the coincidence is that of life imitating art: "queer as fiction, as farce, that their country could happen to be exactly his." But that is the point all along to which his sensitized exilic ambassadorship has taken him. Whether one sees the whole as a comical farce or a queer fiction or an inexorable drama of need and lack, Strether comes imaginatively to a point beyond which his self-limiting capacities will not allow him to act. He finds himself having rejected the sharp facts of Woollett but excluded from the vivid facts of Europe. For the remainder of the action there is a certain pathos in an imagination at its prime served by a prime that will not be his.

If, as James says, Strether lacks both enchantment and enchant-resses before Europe, his own tastes betray his problem. He pur-chases during one of his walks a complete set of Victor Hugo's works. Hugo, the romancer of Paris, is to Strether what Amadis of Gaul was to Don Quixote. Both models ease the move from the sterile plain to the land of verdant romance. Strether is, of course, needful. As James writes of him: "He would have issued, our rueful worthy, from the very heart of New England—at the heels of which matter of course a perfect rain of secrets tumbled for me into the light." One wonders if James has Cervantes's romance-seeking "Knight of the Rueful Countenance" somewhat in mind, especially when in the Gloriani garden scene he describes Strether's epiphany "with the light, with the romance of glory" that "had the conscious-ness of opening to it, for the happy instant, all the windows of his mind, of letting this rather grey interior drink in for once the sun of a clime not marked in his old geography." And Paris is an appropriate exilic geography: "wherever one paused in Paris the imagination reacted before one could stop it." The city is the happy hunting ground for former moralists, a "symbol for more things than had been dreamt of in the philosophy of Woollett."

For Strether, whose imagination is primed, Paris is a field for his projections. James's commentary on this matter in his preface is among the fullest he provides for the book: "It was immeasurable, the opportunity to 'do' a man of imagination." Though he admits it is an imagination in "the minor scale," James immediately goes on to say that minor scale or no, at least the substance of what Strether comes to see and say in the episode set in Gloriani's garden ought to enjoy the advantages of the major since most immediately to the point was the question of that *supplement* of situation logically involved in our gentleman's impulse to deliver himself in the Paris garden on the Sunday afternoon—or if not involved by strict logic then all ideally and enchantingly implied in it. (I say "ideally," because I need scarce mention that for development, for expression of its maximum, my glimmering story was, at the earliest stage, to have nipped the thread of connexion with the possibilities of the actual reported speaker.)

This is fascinating: the major imaginative proclamation about vision is recorded by James as an enchanting supplement to the action of the story, but a supplement that denies the possibilities inherent in it for the one who imagines it. What James calls the supplement therefore belongs to the full life of the novel, if not the missed opportunity for its represented character. As for Strether, he is a part-time worker in the Jamesian enterprise: "it had only been his charming office to project upon that wide field of the artist's vision— which hangs there ever in place like the white sheet suspended for the figures of a child's magic-lantern—a more fantastic and more moveable shadow." The supplement in the artist's world is the primary phenomenon, not an epiphany born of middle-aged male crisis.

This is the essential reason that Strether does not even consider giving in to the temptations of Europe and remaining there as cosmopolitan exile to indulge what might remain for him of sexual life. That strikes him as a violation of both moral and imaginative form. He says to Chad, aghast when the young man suggests that Strether stay in Europe while he goes home to mother: " 'to go back by yourself, I remaining here?' Again for an instant their eyes had the question out; after which Strether said: 'Grotesque!' " *Grotesque* is an intriguing choice of words. The complete plot reversal, so classically worked out, takes on distorted form if Strether should make his impulses the same as his imaginings. What Strether has is what he has fervently argued for, the illusion of freedom; the freedom itself is secondary for him. To choose a course of action that involves, indirectly or not, choosing a woman is to bend Strether's imagination out of shape.

What is of greater moment for James as narrator is the coursing of Strether's imaginative powers into the exilic stream of the narrative so that the arrangement of mimetic instances represents, in a special way, the processes involved in making up a life. As I have been arguing throughout, narrative both imitates action and allegorizes it: "There is the story of one's hero, and then, thanks to the intimate connexion of things, the story of one's story itself." In the latter sense, neither Strether nor Bilham matter to what James calls the supplement in the garden. And the substance of what was said, insofar as it touches on the plot of this story, matters less to James than the power that it reveals for the telling of any story, or the painting of any picture, or the composing of any symphony. The supplement, that is, serves the enterprise in which Strether and Bilham have come to us more than it could or might serve the older and younger men who participate in it.

If the Parisian supplement ends up confusing Strether practically, it at least stimulates him imaginatively. But to experience its benefits he must postpone the material mission at hand. In other words, the action mirrors the aesthetic issue in the book, and, reflexively, the aesthetic issue necessitates the particular form that the action takes. Thus the process begins early when, upon Strether's arrival in Paris, he learns that Mrs. Newsome's letters seem to have been held up. The delay opens supplemental space and time that allows Strether the experience that he will then, in order to buy time for a new mission, record in copious letters back to America in the hope that these, too, will effect delay: "Wasn't he writing against time, and mainly to show he was kind?" His ambassadorial portfolio includes padded reports whose service is not to accomplish the mission that gained him his portfolio but gain time for the mission that will lose him his credentials. For it is a fact of his new Parisian life that he has been cut off from home; the letters stop—Mrs. Newsome utters only a "sacred hush." By this time Strether is aware that his actions constitute imaginative time, which has as its emblem that epiphany in Gloriani's garden, what James called in his "Project" for the book "snatching a little super-sensual hour." Later, when Strether boasts that Chad's turn toward Woollett is "stayed by his own hand," he "had the entertainment of thinking that if he had for that moment stopped the clock it was to promote the next minute this still livelier motion."

The reflex of delay, to which Strether finds himself at least psychologically susceptible from the beginning, is also the reflex of a double consciousness, material and imaginative: "He was burdened, poor Strether—it had better be confessed at the outset—with the oddity of a double consciousness. There was detachment in his zeal and curiosity in his indifference." Detachment from the zeal of his American mission "creates" the time for curiosity to graft onto an original indifference about the lure of the exilic European experience. At the center of all relations is the figure of chiasmus or crossover. Strether soon has a zeal for what he had been curious about and an indifference toward that material comedy from which he had detached himself.

Strether wonders about his new interest in what he considers the "livelier" motion of the action, and his curiosity has a narrative dimension, one that any inventor of plots might contemplate: "Did he live in a false world, a world that had grown simply to suit him?" His is not an idle question for, in a certain sense, the cultivation of the imagination after a long dormancy is *only* for him. In fact, it occurs to Strether that part of his problem is that he invests too much of what he sees in his estimation of other people's conception of reality. That Chad's change, for example, is not noticed by others in the same way he notices it may actually be the menace of the real, as Strether puts it, against the vain or imagined. Later he gets petulant about the possibility: "If they were *all* going to see nothing!" There may be little to see, in terms of the new Woollett delegation to Paris. At best, the American contingent wishes to appropriate Chad's refinements for New England; in other words, the supplementing forces of the exilic experience are themselves put *en exil*.

Strether does not easily give up on the issue of what he has seen and requests that Sarah at least convey to Mrs. Newsome the tenor of the European situation. Sarah marks the aesthetics of his vision, " 'that what you speak of is what *you've* beautifully done.' " And when Strether, in frustration, realizes that his picture of Madame de Vionnet's effort on Chad's behalf is aesthetically uninteresting to the materialist will of Woollett, he virtually begs Sarah for his supplemental image of Marie de Vionnet, if not of Chad: " 'Ah dear Sarah, you must *leave* me this person here!' " She cannot be taken from him, at least in the way he sees her. And he sees her as a piece of exquisite work, the "perfection of art," with "such variety and yet such harmony," "so odd a mixture of lucidity and mystery," part of

Europe's performance, "like Cleopatra in the play, indeed various and multifold."

It is very important for Strether that Madame de Vionnet not only be kept for him in the special way he sees her, but that the pathos in her life that answers to its details of her relation with Chad be kept from him: "while he had himself been enjoying for weeks the view of the brilliant woman's specific action, he just suffered from any characterisation of it by other lips. 'I think tremendously well of her, at the same time that I seem to feel her "life" to be really none of my business.'" Even toward the end, when he realizes "that a creature so fine could be, by mysterious forces, a creature so exploited," it still seems "as if he didn't think of her at all, as if he could think of nothing but the passion, mature, abysmal, pitiful, she represented, and the possibilities she betrayed." It is one thing to say that Strether is simply naively self-protective here, and quite another to say that he knows, after all, that an imaginative view of these things is the best he can make of his present capacities. His steamship ticket may return him to America, but his sensibility, as James implies, has made him a permanent exile; he has crossed over to the land of "difference," and he has "come out on the other side."

The Logic of Delegation in *The Ambassadors*

Julie Rivkin

In his interview with Maria Gostrey at the end of *The Ambassadors,*
Lambert Strether justifies his rejection of her offer with a guiding
principle: "That, you see, is my only logic. Not, out of the whole
affair, to have got anything for myself." Strether's claim—or
disclaimer—sounds like a restatement of that all too familiar ethos of
renunciation that shapes so many of James's terminations. And, in a
sense, it is just that. But in *The Ambassadors,* the ethos of renunciation
takes peculiar force from its link with what is both the novel's subject
and its strategy of composition: ambassadorship. Employing Strether
as ambassador for Mrs. Newsome, James invites us to see Strether's
role as substitute or delegate for another absent authority, James
himself; further, by having Strether invoke a "logic" of delegation
that governs his own actions and permits him no direct profits from
his mission, James implies the existence of a similar textual logic that
regulates the novel's representational system, central to which is
Strether's role as authorial stand-in or delegate. Strether's final
decision should be seen not as an act of personal preference but as
part of a larger textual logic, and this revision requires a shift in the
ground of critical discussion from questions of morality or character
(the realm to which the term *renunciation* belongs) to questions of
representation or delegation. I argue that the ethical issues of the
novel need to be reconsidered from the point of view of what

From *PMLA* 101, no. 5 (October 1986). © 1986 by the Modern Language
Association of America.

Derrida calls the "logic of supplementarity," a logic that governs not only such textual concerns as authority, reference, and intention but also the novel's central thematic conflict between the New England ethos of propriety and property and the Parisian ethos of experience and expenditure.

Derrida works out his representational "logic of the supplement" in his reading of Rousseau in *Of Grammatology*. The supplement, like the ambassador, is a stand-in supposed to alter nothing of that which it stands in for; it is defined as an addition having no effect on the original to which it is being joined. Yet the existence of the addition implies that the original is incomplete and in need of supplementation; the paradoxical logic of supplementarity is that what adds onto also subtracts from, or reveals a lack in, the original. This logic emerges from Derrida's critique of the traditional theory of representation, according to which representation is a secondary copy added onto an original or primary presence, be it of an object or an idea. Writing, for example, is a supplement supposedly added onto an already intact and self-identical speech, which, in the traditional theory, is characterized as a token of pure presence. The supplement of writing is dangerous to speech because writing is not immediately attached to a living presence; it can always go astray, betraying the presence it supposedly communicates. In his critique of this theory, Derrida argues that the ostensible order of priority between speech and writing is in fact reversible, since speech can only function if it uses signs that share a characteristic of writing, detachability from their origin—the capacity to function in the absence of the speaker. The putative original, in other words, could not exist without its copy. Derrida generalizes from this example to all representation and argues that there is no original presence outside supplementation. The presence that is delegated into representation is in a curious way constituted by that representational delegation. The prerepresentational immediacy of the original is, according to Derrida, an illusion, and the advent of the original will always be deferred along a chain of supplements.

> Through this sequence of supplements a necessity is announced: that of an infinite chain, ineluctably multiplying the supplementary mediations that produce the sense of the very thing they defer: the mirage of the thing itself, of immediate presence, of originary perception. Immedi-

acy is derived. That all begins through the intermediary is
what is indeed "inconceivable [to reason]."

(Of Grammatology)

The logic of supplementarity undermines the authority and priority
assigned to the original (the presence of the idea in the mind or of the
thing itself) in the traditional theory of representation. If all representation resembles writing, then originals will always run the risk of
being betrayed by the representations on which they depend for their
own being, of seeing their delegates go astray, generating meanings
and effects that are in no way proper to the original.

The logic of supplementarity bears an uncanny resemblance to
the "logic" traced in *The Ambassadors*; "all begins through the
intermediary" could be the novel's own epigraph. The book literally
begins with the intermediary or ambassador, and the effect of this
beginning is to expose the absence of the very originating authority
he is employed to represent—whether Mrs. Newsome or Henry
James. But if the ambassador betrays his origin in representing it, his
own use of representatives will be subject to the same law. And by
the novel's end he testifies to his comprehension of that necessity
when he speaks of a "logic." Far from invoking moral principle or
personal desire, his explanation of his behavior invokes the representational: it is because he is serving as ambassador and working in
the interests of another that he denies himself experience in his own
person. But interestingly enough the "logic" that requires this
sacrifice justifies all Strether's gains; while an ambassador is not free
to derive profits when in the employ of another, the same law
dictates that an ambassador make use of other ambassadors and
appreciate the accumulations of their own experiences. Strether's
attempt to live vicariously—to live through intermediaries like
Gloriani, little Bilham, and Chad Newsome—simply transfers the
role of ambassador to those around him, thus putting them in exactly
the same bind that his mission for Mrs. Newsome has placed him in.
The logic of delegation, then, is not a principle of renunciation so
much as one of displacement; its effect is to replicate itself, compen-
sating for sacrifices by creating a chain of ambassadors. What this
representational logic leads us to, then, are the experiential difficulties
that constitute the novel's central themes and action: the problem of
missed and vicarious experience; the plot of substitution, deflection,
and deferral; and the novel's dual economy. An economic theory of

representation as the preservation of an original is replaced with a theory of representation as a potentially infinite dispersal of delegates without a guiding origin or authority. And a New England economy of experience as holding in reserve or saving is replaced with a Parisian economy of experience as necessitating an expenditure without reserve, loss without a guaranteed gain. This dual economy accounts for the singular plurality of the novel's title, a plurality dictated by the text's own logic of delegation—not *The Ambassador* but, rather, *The Ambassadors*.

II

Before tracing this logic in the novel, I should like to discuss the preface, where James rewrites the novel's tale of deviation from authority and of mediation of experience as the story of the novel's own composition. More strikingly, the preface does not simply rewrite but reenacts the logic it describes, serving as ambassador for the authority of the text it introduces. Like all Jamesian prefaces, then, this one occupies the classic position of a supplement—purely additional and yet forever reminding us, in James's words, "that one's bag of adventures, conceived or conceivable, has been only half-emptied by the mere telling of one's story." The preface ostensibly completes the project, telling the story that has not been told. But its effect is clearly the opposite: in telling us more, it reminds us of that which is absent; the preface reminds us of an incompleteness that the novel half disguises. By supplementing the novel with the story of its composition, the preface also inevitably hints at the intended novel that never got written. When the author traces the path that moves from initial intention to final realization, he may be more conscious of what he misses than of what he sees:

> As always—since the charm never fails—the retracing of the process from point to point brings back the old illusion. The old intentions bloom again and flower—in spite of all the blossoms they were to have dropped by the way.

As the process continues, the dropped blossoms become more important than those that flowered; what the writer sees is not what is there but what was to have been there: "Cherished intention too inevitably acts and operates, in the book, about fifty times as little as

I had fondly dreamt it might." Like Spencer Brydon in "The Jolly Corner," Henry James in the prefaces is searching for the ghost of the "might have been" and periodically has to remind himself of compensatory satisfactions; the sentence above continues,"but that scarce spoils for me the pleasure of recognising the fifty ways in which I had sought to provide for it."

If cherished intentions must be sacrificed, then James might at least incorporate that principle into his practice; the compositional law he arrives at in the last paragraph of the preface bears a significant relation to the "logic" Strether formulates at the end of his course:

> One would like, at such an hour as this, for critical license, to go into the matter of the noted inevitable deviation (from too fond an original vision) that the exquisite treachery even of the straightest execution may ever be trusted to inflict even on the most mature plan.

"One would like" to do so, but even here, in the preface, one must defer such intentions, sacrificing matter of import and alluding only to the inevitability of such a postponement. James's sentence enacts the compositional law that it discovers, deferring, for perhaps another preface, a full exploration of that "original vision" sacrificed in the execution. Like the Derridean supplement, the Jamesian preface exposes that which is missing in its attempts to complete the story, inviting, in the failure of its own intention, future prefaces, further supplements.

The preface is supplementary in yet another sense explored by Derrida: written after the novel and printed before it, following the novel's composition and yet providing an account of origins, supposedly extrinsic to the text and yet based on it, the preface confounds distinctions between earlier and later, inside and out, of the sort that Strether's ambassadorial voyage also undermines. When pointing out the metaphoric resemblances between preface and novel, one is, of course, tempted to show how the "houses of fiction" and "gardens of life" are "realized" in the tale or how the novel's exchanges enact an economy described in the prefaces. But the chronology of composition suggests a different derivation: the very account of origins that the prefaces provide can be derived from the novels themselves.

The circular derivation of *The Ambassadors*'s origins is particularly striking: James quotes a speech from the novel as the novel's own "germ" or source. As if wary of the compositional story revealed by such a paradigmatic *mise en abyme,* James then tells an alternative story, emphasizing how the speech was taken from real life. In this second account, James claims that the germ was given him "bodily . . . by the spoken word" and adds that he took "the image over exactly as [he] happened to have met it." But even in this account, the emphasis on physical presence, speech, and duplication is belied by the sentence that follows: "A friend had repeated to me, with great appreciation, a thing or two said to him by a man of distinction, much his senior, and to which a sense akin to that of Strether's melancholy eloquence might be imputed." In place of duplication, we have repetition with "appreciation" (a term that always carries economic resonances in James); in place of direct speech and bodily presence, we have quotation: these are the words of another, spoken in a different place by a man of a different age. The original moment is already at one remove from its origin; the young man who repeats the words of another is himself an ambassador or intermediary, and the original speech is itself a quotation. It is the final phrase, though, that puts before us the fictional status of origins: if a "sense akin to that of Strether's melancholy eloquence" must be "imputed" to these words, has not Strether's speech become the origin for this one, rather than the reverse?

What the preface, in fact, presents is a double story of the novel's composition. To the degree that it reveals the impossibility of fixing origins, it proclaims a sure foundation for the novel; in the words of the reviser, there was "never one of those alarms as for a suspected hollow beneath one's feet, a felt ingratitude in the scheme adopted, under which confidence fails and opportunity seems but to mock." While at one point James laments "the exquisite treachery even of the straightest execution," he earlier insists, "Nothing resisted, nothing betrayed." The preface opens, "Nothing is easier to state than the subject of *The Ambassadors,*" but it goes on not to state but to locate the subject. The centrality of the location is striking— the subject can be found in the novel's formal center ("in the second chapter of Book Fifth . . . planted or 'sunk' . . . in the centre of the current"), in its geographical and by extension existential center ("in Gloriani's garden" in the center of Paris), and in the novel's own "germ"; however, the emphasis on centrality should not disguise for us this first act of displacement. The preface closes by acknowledging the inevitability of displacement and deviation, but in the beginning it insists on the directness of the novel's growth: "Never can a composition of this sort have sprung straighter from a dropped grain of suggestion, and never can that grain, developed, overgrown and smothered, have yet lurked more in the mass as an independent particle." The rhetorical balance of this sentence suggests a correspondence not only betweeen part and whole, "grain" and "mass," but also between composition and interpretation; the straight growth of the whole composition from the original part determines the direct perception of the original part in the mass. The compositional story coincident with this organic figure of "germ" and "growth" is as far from the logic of the intermediary as we can imagine; indeed, to suggest that the grain can be found in the mass as easily as the mass can grow from the grain is to deny both deviation from one's intentions and the inevitability of loss over time.

Not surprisingly, the contradictions of the compositional story are those of the novel; the preface puts itself in a "false position" much like the one in which it finds its protagonist. The compositional story and the protagonist's story intersect with particular intensity in the novel's "germ," where the contradictions noted above appear with full thematic resonance. Indeed, the germ directly challenges the assumptions implicit in its own organic metaphor. Far from suggesting that intentions can be realized in a process as natural and unimpeded as the "straight growth" of a plant, the germ itself conveys not only the deviant course taken in executing intentions but also the inevitability of a certain failure in the attempt. Instead of supporting that easy match between part and whole, composition and interpretation suggested by the natural analogy, the germ is presented as a mismatch, a "crisis." "The idea of the tale," James points out, "resides indeed in the very fact that an hour of such unprecedented ease should have been felt by him [Strether] *as* a crisis, and he is at pains to express it for us as neatly as we could desire." The expression takes the form of the following speech:

> Live all you can; it's a mistake not to. It doesn't so much matter what you do in particular so long as you have your life. If you haven't had that what *have* you had? I'm too old—too old at any rate for what I see. What one loses one loses; make no mistake about that. Still, we have the illusion of freedom; therefore don't, like me to-day, be without the memory of that illusion. I was either, at the

right time, too stupid or too intelligent to have it, and now I'm a case of reaction against the mistake. Do what you like so long as you don't make it. For it *was* a mistake. Live, live!

This speech, appearing as it is quoted in the preface, sets in peculiar relief the compositional success story with which the preface opens. It does not promise an easy recovery of the past, or a neat correspondence between part and whole; rather, it presents a new version of the logic of delegation. This moment of retrospection—claimed in the preface to constitute the "germ," "essence," and "centre" of The Ambassadors—deconstructs the notions of origins and unmediated experience that it supposedly embodies. Its particular bad faith is that it confesses the impossibility of the very success it recommends for another. When the speech (in a somewhat more expansive form) appears in the novel, delivered to the exquisitely sensitive little Bilham, this bad faith seems even more pronounced. The "freedom" to live that Strether urges for his young friend is knowingly presented as an illusion; in wishing he had "the memory of that illusion" himself, Strether denies the possibility of any such illusions to the young man who stands before him. The urgency of Strether's "Live, live!" is at odds with his conviction that the freedom to live is illusory. But if in the act of delegating this mission to "live," Strether both acknowledges and attempts to evade the logic of delegation, little Bilham is "too intelligent" to deceive himself. Little Bilham's response to the injunction to "live" demonstrates not only the inevitability of this logic of deflected intentions and mediated experience but also his acceptance of the stance of ambassador; if on the one hand little Bilham turns "quite solemn, and . . . this was a contradiction of the innocent gaiety the speaker had wished to promote," on the other hand he replies, "Oh but I don't know what I want to be, at your age, too different from you!" While Strether's speech is supposedly designed to invite a course of development different from his own, it acknowledges the impossibility of that which it recommends, and acknowledges it to someone who in fact anticipates just such a course of necessary deviation—and just such an act of future retrospection.

Distinctive as the tone of this speech is, it should already sound familiar to us: Strether's tone on reexamining the course of his life sounds much like James's on reexamining the course of his novel—

specifically in those moments when he links success to failure and exposes the fiction of origins. Just as Strether regrets not the freedom of youth but the illusion of freedom, James himself can only regret the intentions he had "fondly dreamt" might have been realized in the novel. In view of his claim that the novel is "frankly, quite the best, 'all round,' of my productions," James's focus on its mistakes has peculiar impact. For in *The Ambassadors* mistakes are intimately connected to successes. Not only does James make his story out of the deflection of Strether's original intentions, but the novel's subject and "germ" is a moment of retrospection that predicts the inevitability of such deflection. Of his novel, James says, "The book, . . . critically viewed, is touchingly full of these disguised and repaired losses, these insidious recoveries, these intensely redemptive consistencies." If we substitute Strether for James and "my life" for "the book," we return to a statement very like Strether's speech to little Bilham. James's attitude, on rereading his most successful book, is reminiscent of Strether's on reviewing the less successful text of his life; the moment of retrospection that James quotes as the novel's origin predicts his own response in his moment of retrospection about the novel itself.

If James sounds like Strether in his general sense of the inevitability of deviation from design, he is even more closely linked to his ambassador in the particular deviation he chooses to mention in the preface. First, he emphasizes that his "law" of representation necessitates such compromises; that is, it is largely because he can present the world only as mediated by his authorial delegate that he is constrained to depart from his original design. The one compromise that he singles out for mention reveals even more compellingly the operation of this law: "one of the suffered treacheries had consisted precisely, for Chad's whole figure and presence, of a direct presentability diminished and compromised." James's selection of Chad as the locus of his own regret repeats the regret of his delegate, Strether; Chad figures for Strether as the person who, even more than little Bilham, is free to "live" without mediation, much as Chad figures for his author as one who could embody "presence," were he only seen directly. But "direct presentability," like unmediated experience, is illusory—even if the failure of the illusion is suffered as treachery. What James attempts and regrets with Chad is like what Strether attempts and regrets with both Chad and little Bilham; in confining his preface to the ostensibly formal problems of composition and representation, James finds himself at the heart of the experiential difficulties that plague his fictional representative. More-over, James's response to this representational challenge—"the whole economy of his author's relation to him [Chad] has at important points to be redetermined"—suggests the revisions in the economy that govern the similarly mediated relation between the authority of Mrs. Newsome and her son, Chad, revisions that, after all, constitute the plot of *The Ambassadors*.

III

The ambassadorial logic that is inscribed in the preface and that links the story of the story so inextricably to the story of the hero regulates all the novel's transactions, from the linguistic to the economic, from the familial to the cultural. Hired to mediate between mother and son, between American and European cultural and economic practices, Strether is asked to perform a mission that restores propriety as much as property, sexual as well as commercial fidelity. Returning the wayward son to his mother, the irresponsible heir to the family business, the illicit lover to the legally sanctioned marriage—all should follow from the literal communication of the message that the ambassador carries. Literality is the linguistic form of fidelity; if language could be kept from deviating into figuration, if messages could suffer no change in transmission, then the ambas-sador's errand of restoration might succeed. But the fate of the words that Strether carries—those "Boston 'really's' " and "virtuous attach-ments" that attempt to fix words to referents only to open up abysses of ambiguity—suggests both the infidelities of language toward the experience to which it supposedly corresponds and the possible promiscuities harbored in the novel's relationships themselves. What such linguistic aberrations demonstrate is that the fidelity Mrs. Newsome demands is at odds with the means she employs; the terms of the ambassador's engagement with Mrs. Newsome become the terms under which that engagement is betrayed. Instead of fixing New England categories on Parisian experience, then, Strether discovers that infidelities and deviations characterize his "straight" New England errand from the outset. The ambassador cannot come home to either proper behavior or literal meaning; rather, he remains the figure for the necessary figurative turns and errors that accom-pany all acts of exchange and representation. In his own about-face—

as he shifts from representing the interests of Mrs. Newsome to representing those of Mme de Vionnet—he suggests the reversal to which all the novel's representational terms are subject; he deconstructs, rather than preserves, the novel's structuring oppositions of domestic and foreign, proper and improper, legal and illicit on which the New England values depend.

It is necessary irony that Mrs. Newsome, the figure who sets this representational logic in motion, is the one least able to acknowledge its existence. As the absent authority who stands behind all the novel's ambassadors, she sends her delegates off with the express understanding that they alter nothing of that for which they stand in. She wants a representative who can fill in for her, maintain a likeness, without a difference, who can deliver the message she speaks "to the letter." Were she to enunciate her theory of representation, it would resemble those passages in the preface where James speaks of straight growth, direct speech, and exact replication. Although she makes use of ambassadors, she assumes that her business will be carried out as it would be in person; her fixity of purpose makes it impossible for her to imagine any shift or deviation. After taking the measure of his own deviation in the performance of his ambassadorial mission, Strether comments:

> That's just her difficulty—that she doesn't admit surprises. It's a fact that, I think, describes and represents her; and it falls in with what I tell you—that she's all, as I've called it, fine cold thought. She had, to her own mind, worked the whole thing out in advance, and worked it out for me as well as for herself. Whenever she has done that, you see, there's no room left; no margin, as it were, for any alteration.

Given her assumption and attitudes, it is particularly ironic that Mrs. Newsome must resort to using ambassadors to realize her conception. The ambassador is just the "margin for alteration" that she does not acknowledge.

But the absolutism of Mrs. Newsome's authority complements the deviations of her ambassadors; had she not "worked the whole thing out in advance . . . for [Strether] as well as for herself," she would not experience ambassadorial revision as a complete betrayal of her design. Were the fidelity she demanded less than complete, were the specific terms of her plan's execution left to the improvisations of her ambassador, she could accommodate the alterations incurred in the act of execution. In remaining outside the novel's sphere of ambassadorial representation and attempting to maintain complete control over it, she renders herself vulnerable to its logic, dependent on it, present only in the persons of her ambassadors, who by necessity differ from her and thereby misrepresent her.

If Mrs. Newsome can be seen as almost a parody of the absent author who "works the whole thing out in advance" only to find the scheme revised in the act of execution, then Maria Gostrey can be seen as the expert on the ambassadorial logic that will substitute for Mrs. Newsome's authority. The novel's first chapter serves as Strether's introduction to this logic of revision and substitution, and appropriately enough, Maria Gostrey is herself not only a substitute for the figure that Strether expects—Waymarsh—but also what James calls a *ficelle,* a supplementary figure in the compositional story. The novel opens, famously, with Strether's first question concerning the whereabouts of his friend Waymarsh, and it is only because his friend is not there that Strether finds himself in the company of this alternative acquaintance. The wandering walk that they take through Chester suggests the deviant course that results from any act of substitution, be it representational or ambassadorial, and by the time Strether encounters Waymarsh at the end of the chapter, he has traveled a path that leads far from Waymarsh's straight and narrow way of propriety.

Maria Gostrey's revisionary impact on Strether's plans parallels her impact on James's design in the compositional story; she is a substitute not only for the figure Strether awaits but also for the one James had planned. In the "project" for the novel, Strether was to meet Maria Gostrey only after he met Waymarsh, and indeed only through Waymarsh's acquaintance. This revision suggests the common representational logic that binds the compositional story to the fictional one; the novel can only begin as a substitute for the design that ostensibly serves as its origin, just as Strether's experience as a delegate can only begin as a turn away from his plan. James's other revision of the novel's "project" further stresses deviation as a principle of narrative development; in changing "Way*mark*" to "Way*marsh,*" James suggests not only the inevitable changes that come in the course of execution but also the transformation of severity into uncertainty and the breakdown of proper boundaries that is the fate of New England in the novel. Maria Gostrey—her name falls one consonant short of "go straight" and leaves us with the open-ended sound and open path of "go stray"—comes between Strether and Waymarsh and in this act of mediation opens up a way for Strether that is far from the course he intended to travel.

What Maria Gostrey has to teach Strether about ambassadorial logic begins as a response to the practical social problem they face as strangers desiring to make each other's acquaintance and eventually leads into an exploration of the premises on which Strether's mission is based. Though James's preface describes her function as eliciting "certain indispensable facts" about Strether in a form that allows James to treat the otherwise "inserted block of merely referential narrative" in entertainingly scenic form, she exposes the "facts" as something other than factual and the "referential narrative" as oddly detached from reference. This critique of the referential begins with her first words. Echoing the hotel receptionist who has just produced a telegram from Strether's absent friend Waymarsh, she is "moved to ask, by his leave, if it were possibly a question of Mr. Waymarsh of Milrose Connecticut—Mr. Waymarsh the American lawyer." Although she ostensibly seeks to attach Strether's friend's identity to a fixed point of geographical and professional reference, the name "Waymarsh" serves as a mere pretext for conversation, less important as a designation than as the vehicle of a certain effect. The unimportance of Maria Gostrey's reference emerges when she substitutes another name for that of Waymarsh. Asked whether he knows the Munsters, Strether is compelled to admit that he does not, but, interestingly enough, the name of someone that he does not know serves just as well as the name of someone he does to provide a basis for this new connection. Under the guise of offering references, Maria Gostrey exposes the precariousness of such foundations; proper names, far from being the rigid designators Strether's New England sense of propriety would have trained him to expect, begin to operate instead as intermediaries loosened from reference. In his absence "Waymarsh" legitimizes relations that he himself might not authorize in person, suggesting the fate of that other character who appears in the novel in name alone: "Mrs. Newsome."

The proper names that pose the greatest difficulties for Strether and Maria Gostrey are, of course, not "Waymarsh" and "Munster" but their own. Faced with the social problem of providing introductions when they have no basis for their new acquaintance, they find themselves relying on calling cards. But though Strether pockets

Maria Gostrey's card as if it were the person it names (he finds it "positively droll . . . that he should already have Maria Gostrey, whoever she was—of which he hadn't really the least idea—in a place of safe keeping"), Maria Gostrey's mistaking of Strether's card for her own links the interchangeability of cards to the interchangeability of other representations. Like the cards they carry as tokens of their identity, these two ambassadors are, they discover, also detachable from a fixed ground of reference.

Maria Gostrey's continuing investigations into the background of her new friend only reveal further the precarious foundation on which his identity rests. His profession is not more fixed than his name. Strether speaks to Maria Gostrey of his position as editor of a journal:

> "Woollett has a Review—which Mrs. Newsome, for the most part, magnificently pays for and which I, not at all magnificently, edit. My name's on the cover. . . ."
>
> "And what kind of a Review is it?". . .
>
> "Well, it's green."
>
> "Do you mean in political colour as they say here—in thought?"
>
> "No; I mean the cover's green—of the most lovely shade."

Strether's comic insistence on the literal in the face of Maria Gostrey's more convincing figurative interpretation of his words suggests that he fears such deviations into the metaphoric will lead him to stray from propriety. But in substituting cover for content, pigment for point of view, he exposes what he tries to conceal. Strether's joke of identifying the book by its cover is more serious than it might appear, for it bears directly on his identity: "He was Lambert Strether because he was on the cover, whereas it should have been, for anything like glory, that he was on the cover because he was Lambert Strether." The names printed on calling cards are like this name printed on the review; instead of being based on some preexisting and prerepresentational referent, Strether's identity derives from its publication. The text that advertises his public identity also creates it.

In principle, Woollett, Massachusetts, epitomizes proper identity and proper behavior, a literal world untouched by compromising metaphors. When Maria Gostrey asks, for example, "Who in the world's Jim Pocock?" Strether replies, "Why Sally's husband. That's the only way we distinguish people at Woollett." According to the "Woollett standard," as Strether will call it later, the Newsome family stands as an absolute, the source of all "distinction," both designation and value. Other residents are distinguished—both known and seen as worthy—by their relation to the Newsomes. But Maria Gostrey senses a "cover" even here. As she explores the origins of the Newsome clan, she comes on a foundation as dubious as any that she and Strether have just invented for their own connection. On Maria Gostrey's questioning, Strether divulges, "The source of [Chad's] grandfather's wealth—and thereby of his own share in it—was not particularly noble." Asked further about the source, Strether can only reply, "Well—practices. . . . I shan't describe *him* nor narrate his exploits." Maria Gostrey remarks, "Lord, what abysses!" The "Woollett standard" turns out to be founded on an abyss, the source of all value to be something unspeakable. Strether says, "The men I speak of—they did as everyone does; and (besides being ancient history) it was all a matter of appreciation." In place of some grounded and morally proper origin for inherited wealth, Maria Gostrey discovers a supplementary process of accumulation or "appreciation." Through her questions about the figures—both personal and monetary—that stand behind Strether, Maria Gostrey deconstructs the literal system of designation Woollett supposedly embodies by tracing it back to the "unspeakable."

"Ancient history" is, in fact, no different from the present story. All parties stand to gain by Chad's return—the Newsomes in wealth, Strether in marriage. But these "appreciations" are also hidden by covers. When Maria Gostrey asks Strether, "Then how do they distinguish *you?*" he sidesteps the question that would have obliged him to confess that he stood to gain from his mission. "They *don't*— except, as I've told you, by the green cover." But clearly Strether's "distinction" in the world of Woollett is to inhere in being Mrs. Newsome's husband. So Maria Gostrey is correct to sense that the "green cover" is a cover in another sense: "The green cover won't— nor will *any* cover—avail you with *me*. You're of a depth of duplicity!" Again Maria Gostrey turns to the metaphoric in her critique of this New England "straight talk," which lays claim to disinterested moral probity and strict literality. What she draws out is the necessity of metaphors or figures to the supposedly prefigural, "virtuous," and uncompromised world of Woollett. Indeed, the town's propriety, like the identity behind proper names, seems to depend on representations, metaphors that create an effect of propriety but that designate no fixed literal referent.

As she explores the grounds of Strether's ambassadorship, then, Maria Gostrey begins to confound the simple distinctions between literal and figurative, proper and improper, America and Europe, on which his mission apparently rests. In questioning proper names, Maria Gostrey is also questioning the origins of property and, by extension, of Mrs. Newsome's rights of ownership over both her ambassador, Strether, and her son, Chad. She exposes as problematic both the origin of the Newsome fortune and the mother's absolute authority, thereby questioning Mrs. Newsome's assumptions about representation as exact replication. She replaces the New England conservative economy and retentive theory of representation with an economy that encourages extravagance and a model of representation as deviation from a source. As a "general guide," "a sort of superior 'courier-maid,' " "a companion at large"—apart from being James's own *ficelle*—she not only stands for a principle of ambassadorial representation as "going astray"; she also knows the ambassadorial economy that offers no return on one's investment. In words that anticipate Strether's final recognition, she acknowledges, "I don't do it, you know, for any particular advantage. I don't do it, for instance—some people do, you know—for money." From the initial violations of propriety to the exposure of property, Maria Gostrey signals that the ambassador's fate is inevitably a straying from authority, as well as a departure from the logic of investment as personal gain.

IV

When Strether arrives in Paris, his first impulse is to establish contact with Mrs. Newsome, as if to correct himself for the deviant explorations he has already embarked on with Maria Gostrey. But just as proper names led into an investigation of improprieties, so now the letters that Strether seeks as a link with authority will become the marks of his distance with the Woollett standard that is his source. Much like his effort to meet Waymarsh before embarking on European explorations, his attempt to take up his correspondence with Mrs. Newsome is also baffled by an absence—her letters have not yet arrived. And when the letters do come the next day, Strether has already displaced himself from his New England basis.

Literally, this displacement is traced in his restless wanderings from the bank at Rue Scribe, where the letters arrive, to the "penny chair" in the Luxembourg Gardens where he finally reads them; figuratively, he has enacted a shift from a New England economy of equal exchange (the bank) to a Parisian economy of expenditure (the penny chair). Moreover, this shift in economy is a shift in the concept of representation: while Mrs. Newsome's letters give him "chapter and verse for the moral that nothing would suffer" in his absence, telling him "who would take up this and who take up that exactly where he had left it," he has come to discover that his act of replacement and displacement makes such scriptural literalism no longer possible. He reflects, "It was the difference, the difference of being just where he was and *as* he was, that formed the escape—this difference was so much greater than he had dreamed it would be; and what he finally sat there turning over was the strange logic of his finding himself so free." What the letters from Mrs. Newsome trace in their journey from bank to garden is Strether's shift from the rigors of New England authority to the pleasures of Parisian experience. But what Strether has yet to discover is that the representational "logic" that governs his relation to authority will also govern his relation to Parisian experience. Though Strether rather comically wonders, "Was he to renounce all amusement for the sweet sake of that authority? . . . [A]lmost any acceptance of Paris might give one's authority away," neither "authority" nor "Paris" is his simply for the bartering.

Operative in Strether's reckoning is the American conception that Paris embodies "experience" in as unmediated and direct a fashion as Mrs. Newsome herself embodies authority. Though Strether, with his elaborate scruples about participation, might seem to escape such a simplification, the care with which he confines his indulgences to the vicarious confesses to his acceptance of the American myth of Paris. While the choice to live vicariously might seem to acknowledge a necessarily mediated relation to experience, it actually bases itself on just the opposite perception. Life or experience is there to be had, even if Strether cannot enjoy it in person. Strether's image of Paris confirms this conviction: behind the city's manifold appearances there is a reality to which those in the know have access. Though he is compelled to admit that in this city "parts

were not to be discriminated nor differences comfortably marked
. . . what seemed all surface one moment seemed all depth the next,"
he still thinks of penetrating facades, touching bottom, and arriving
at the "truth." Whether his emphasis is metaphysical (presence, life)
or epistemological (the truth), he conceives of "experience" as a goal
that can be reached, a prize that can be won—if not by himself, then
by another.

The "other" who has been posited from the start as occupying
a privileged relation to Parisian experience is Chad Newsome; and
just as it is initially Chad whom Strether must rescue and protect
from that experience, it will later be Chad through whom Strether
will imagine his own vicarious access to that experience. These
contradictory responses share an assumption: that Chad is in "life" in
a way that Strether can only imagine. Strether's first meeting with
Chad is critical in establishing this privileged relation to Parisian
experience, even as it marks Strether's separation from anything like
a New England point of origin. In particular, Strether's peculiar
response to the changes in Chad—what Strether calls "this sharp
rupture of an identity"—and the immediacy with which this rupture
translates into a disconnection between Chad and his "New England
female parent" allow Strether to see the new Chad as the product of
a different origin, the Parisian experience that Strether now sees as
his own goal. Speculating to Maria Gostrey about the source of these
changes, he says, "Well, the party responsible is, I suppose, the fate
that waits for one, the dark doom that rides. . . . One wants,
confound it, don't you see? . . . one wants to enjoy anything so rare.
Call it then life . . . call it poor dear old life simply that springs the
surprise." In naming this source life, Strether suggests that, if the
authority of Mrs. Newsome has been challenged, it has been
supplanted by an equally absolute agency of experience.

Although Strether's new Parisian friends confirm his impression
of Chad's improvements, they qualify Strether's sense that the
change has been absolute. And in doing so, they challenge his
conceptual model of experience. Maria Gostrey warns Strether,
"He's not so good as you think!" and little Bilham echoes the doubt:
Chad is "like the new edition of an old book that one has been fond
of—revised and amended, brought up to date, but not quite the thing
one knew and loved." Little Bilham's metaphor of the revised book
substitutes for Strether's notion of experience as an absolute concealed behind its representative, Chad. Strether's attempt to find the

"truth" about Chad, for example, has just this structure. "Are you engaged to be married—is that your secret?—to the young lady?" Strether asks Chad. The response—"I have no secret—though I may have secrets!"—challenges Strether's model of a single explanatory reality behind all appearances. A later conversation with Mme de Vionnet makes this difference even more explicit; advised by Mme de Vionnet that he should simply tell Mrs. Newsome the truth, Strether is moved to inquire, "And what do you call the truth?" Again, Mme de Vionnet not only refuses to give the expected answer but also revises the assumptions of the question: "Well, *any* truth—about us all—that you see yourself."

If Maria Gostrey teaches Strether that ambassadorial representatives go astray in the absence of their guiding New England authority—thus teaching him something about all representation—the Parisians teach him that the experience, the truth of life, that he imagined stood behind representatives like Chad is also something detached from any fixed ground, something that, like Chad, might be revisable according to one's perspective and that, like Mme de Vionnet, might be multiple rather than unique, singular, and distinct. But what Maria Gostrey could only tell Strether, suggesting that he was already participating in the phenomenon without knowing it, he learns for himself in Gloriani's garden. There, it becomes clear that the revisionary process he has already begun to experience, the process of substitution and deviation he has been embarked on from the novel's opening sentence, is in fact the life he has been seeking. Thinking he stands outside, like Mrs. Newsome, holding in reserve, he in fact is already in the middle of a new economy of representation and exchange, caught in the logic that requires multiple delegates and expenditure without return.

This revisionary process may have been evident from Strether's first steps in Chester, but the potential for change takes on climactic force in Gloriani's garden, a setting that promises Strether a vision not only of Parisian life at its most exclusive but also of the particular "life" behind Chad's miraculous transformation. Here, at the heart of the novel, in the heart of Paris, Strether stands off to one side, wondering as he watches those who belong to the "great world" whether "he himself, for the moment and thus related to them by his observation, [was] *in* it?" The vision in the garden shows experience to be the product or effect of a juxtaposition of representations, rather than the revelation of some truth of presence or experience that stands as a ground behind the world of appearances. Indeed, Strether—by juxtaposing and comparing himself to others he desires to be "like," by sending forth delegates like little Bilham to catch their naive notions of life, and by endlessly revising his own perceptions—shows himself to be already thoroughly in the middle (an intermediary without anchor, authority, or goal) of that which he seeks, its living embodiment or ambassador.

Standing in the garden with little Bilham, Strether says, "I know, if we talk of that—whom *I* should enjoy being like!" Following Strether's line of vision, focused now on an encounter taking place in the center of the garden between his host Gloriani and a woman of the world, little Bilham guesses at his allusion: "Gloriani?" As the scene alters, though, so does Strether's desire, so that while he might have begun with Gloriani in mind, by the time he has finished speaking he finds that a different figure has been interposed. Between his initial wish and his final claim, or between little Bilham's guess—"Gloriani?"—and Strether's answer, this other vision grows:

> He had just made out, in the now full picture, something and somebody else; another impression had been superimposed. A young girl in a white dress and a softly plumed white hat had suddenly come into view, and what was presently clear was that her course was toward them. What was clearer still was that the handsome young man at her side was Chad Newsome, and what was clearest of all was that she was therefore Mademoiselle de Vionnet, that she was unmistakeably pretty—bright gentle shy happy wonderful—and that Chad now, with a consummate calculation of effect, was about to present her to his old friend's vision. What was clearest of all indeed was something much more than this, something at the single stroke of which—and wasn't it simply juxtaposition?—all vagueness vanished. It was the click of a spring—he saw the truth. He had by this time also met Chad's look; there was more of it in that; and the truth, accordingly, so far as Bilham's enquiry was concerned, had thrust in the answer. "Oh Chad!"—it was that rare youth he should have enjoyed being "like."

Although Strether believes he has found his ideal ambassador and his image of life incarnate at the heart of the Parisian garden, his conviction is countered by its status as a revision of his own intention, a revision that shifts the meaning of his words in the very moment of their utterance. Moreover, the picture itself—as fixed and complete as Strether might wish it to be—exposes its own revisionary potential in the very demonstration of its plenitude. He desires a New England literality, but he is given a Parisian process of substitution, deviation, and revision. Though the emphasis is on immediacy and presence—the picture is "now full"; the "truth" suddenly clear "before him" and "present" to "his vision"—there are symptoms of inadequacy, displacement, and supplementation. For example, in the very "now" of revelation (twice repeated), Strether sees something "more" in Chad's look, an invitation to supplements that Strether might prefer to ignore. Similarly, the sequence of adjectives that mark the process of clarification— "clear," "clearer still," "clearest of all," "clearest of all indeed"— adds something "more" at the moment it should be complete: the repetition of the superlative suggests that the ultimate can be superseded, that the superlative itself is simply a product of comparison. Indeed, comparison—or "juxtaposition"—turns out to be the source of Strether's vision of truth; in seeing Chad next to Gloriani, and Mlle de Vionnet next to Chad, Strether perceives an ideal "likeness" between himself and Chad. But if truth is a product of juxtaposition rather than a revelation of an absolute, there is no reason that truth should stop here, for different juxtapositions will give rise to different truths. And truth does not stop here: as convinced as Strether is that he has discovered in Jeanne de Vionnet the living source of Chad's mysterious enrichment (and thereby in the "rare youth" his own chosen delegate), this truth will quickly dissolve in the face of further juxtaposition. But the point is not that Strether gets it wrong in guessing Chad is involved with Jeanne de Vionnet when Chad is actually involved with Jeanne's mother; nor is it that Strether is wrong in guessing that Chad's attachment is "virtuous" in the New England sense of the word when it is actually adulterous. Rather, what Strether will discover as he replaces one truth about experience with another is that there is no stopping point in this logic of revision, no superlative that will stand beyond all comparison, no originating intention that can hold its meaning fixed to the ultimate referent. Just as authority will find intention revised in the act of representation, so too one representative will give way to another, one apparently "full picture" will be "superimposed" by another.

Gloriani's garden encourages Strether's myth of Parisian life as a fully present plenitude only to expose it as an effect of supplementarity, of possibly endless substitutions; instead of a presence that gives rise to delegational representations, life turns out to be an effect of the interplay or juxtaposition of representatives. Indeed, Chad is "life" in that he is associated with a "consummate calculation of effect," a product of representation rather than a ground standing behind it. Though Strether anxiously wonders whether things show "for what they really are," his New England conception of identity as a stable reality behind appearances is giving way to a Parisian conception of identity as a product and function of appearances.

The person who comes most to epitomize the life that Strether has been seeking through delegational representatives like Chad, the presence of experience that stands behind all those intersubstitutable and supplementary representatives as a stable referent, ground, or origin to which they point and from which they derive their meaning, as Strether does from Mrs. Newsome, is Mme de Vionnet. Yet what Strether discovers is that the life that seemed to stand outside the logic of supplementary delegation is itself subject to its laws. Mme de Vionnet turns out to represent life as something far more problematic, supplementary, and plural than Strether's New England categories anticipated. She is lacking but, by virtue of that, rich in supplementary possibilities: though on first meeting her he notes that "there was somehow not quite a wealth in her; and a wealth was all that, in his simplicity, he had definitely prefigured," he will later find her "like Cleopatra in the play, indeed various and multifold." As one of the Parisian cognoscenti will put it, "She's fifty women." Strether, anxious about the instability such excesses imply, insists, "Ah but only one . . . at a time." The response refuses to pacify: "Perhaps. But in fifty times—!"

Thus, what Mme de Vionnet comes to reveal is that behind representation there is no firm ground. The supplements that make up representation, delegation, ambassadorship are potentially infinite. Indeed, she confirms what Strether had already begun to learn from Maria Gostrey—that property (as the self of proper names, the wealth of family, the propriety of behavior, and the presence that stands behind representation) is itself an effect, a product of the interplay of likenesses and likelihoods, the intersubstitution of representations. In Mme de Vionnet's world, there are no final authorities of the sort Mrs. Newsome claims to be; there are only ambassadors. Moreover, by displacing the economy of representation that governed Strether's initial conception of experience, Mme de Vionnet also displaces the economy of commercial transaction that governed his initial conception of his mission. Though Mrs. Newsome would have her ambassador hold fast to a single identity as her representative—and receive his promised reward in fair exchange—Strether learns from Mme de Vionnet a freely disseminated selfhood that asks for no return. The new economy is not all celebratory: as Mme de Vionnet acknowledges about her relationship with Chad, loss is the only certainty. But it is her economy rather than Mrs. Newsome's that accounts for Strether's final gesture. In renouncing profit, he renounces a New England system of representation and a New England exchange rate. But the logic that requires that renunciation is the logic that gives him the freedom to deviate and revise, to become fifty ambassadors if need be, even if only one at a time.

Chronology

1843	Henry James born April 15 in New York City to Henry James, a gentleman-scholar, and Mary Walsh James. Family moves to London.
1844–45	James's father suffers nervous breakdown, becomes a Swedenborgian. Family lives in London and Paris.
1845–55	Family lives in New York, chiefly New York City, where senior James's friends such as Ralph Waldo Emerson, Bronson Alcott, Horace Greeley, and William Cullen Bryant frequently visit. Henry James, Jr., attends various schools in the city, until father decides he and siblings should have European educations.
1855–59	Family lives in Europe—children educated by tutor and private school in several countries. James contracts typhoid. In 1858, family returns and settles in Newport, Rhode Island. James makes friends with Thomas Sergeant Perry, who attends Berkeley Institute with him, and with John La Farge.
1859–60	James family returns to Europe, where Henry attends Institution Rochette, a pre-engineering school in Geneva. Soon withdraws and enrolls in Academy (later University of Geneva) with brother William to study literature. Studies German in Bonn.
1860–62	Family returns to Newport. William studies under William Morris Hunt and Henry sits in. They both attend Frank Sanborn's experimental school in Concord, Massachusetts, favored by the Transcendentalists.
1861	Orphaned Temple cousins come to live with family in Newport. Henry becomes close to Minnie Temple.

	William leaves study of art, takes up science. Henry suffers back injury during a fire.
1862–63	Attends Harvard Law School. Brothers Garth Wilkinson James and Robertson James join black Union regiments during Civil War; Wilkinson badly wounded.
1864	Family moves to Boston. James publishes first (unsigned) story, "A Tragedy of Error," in *Continental Monthly*. Begins writing reviews for *North American Review*.
1865	Publishes signed story, "The Story of a Year," in the *Atlantic Monthly*. Begins to write reviews for the *Nation*.
1866–68	Family moves to Cambridge, Massachusetts; James continues to publish reviews and stories. Friendship with William Dean Howells.
1869–70	James returns to Europe for Grand Tour; meets several Pre-Raphaelites, Darwin, and George Eliot while in England. Minnie Temple dies of tuberculosis a month before James returns to America.
1871	*Watch and Ward* and "A Passionate Pilgrim" published in the *Atlantic Monthly*. Tours northeastern United States to write travel sketches for the *Nation*.
1872–74	Returns to Europe, accompanying sister Alice and aunt Kate on tour. Continues writing stories and travel sketches for the *Nation,* this time of Europe through American eyes, from which he now earns enough to support himself. Friendship with James Russell Lowell, Fanny Kemble, and William Wetmore Story. Travels around Italy with William; returns to America with nearly complete manuscript of *Roderick Hudson*.
1875	*Roderick Hudson* appears, first serially in the *Atlantic Monthly,* then as book. Publishes *A Passionate Pilgrim and Other Tales; Transatlantic Sketches*. Moves to Paris, where he will write European letters for the *New York Tribune*.
1876	Turgenev introduces James to Flaubert, who introduces him to Zola, Daudet, de Maupassant, Doré, de Goncourt, and other French intellectuals. Resigns from the *Tribune* job because editor wants too much gossip. Moves to London, where he will live for the next ten

years. Serialization of *The American* in the *Atlantic Monthly* (book published 1877).

1878   *French Poets and Novelists* published in England; *The Europeans* serialized in the *Atlantic Monthly*. "Daisy Miller" appears in Leslie Stephen's *Cornhill Magazine*—the foreign publication costs James his American rights and it is pirated in the United States. Elected to Reform Club.

1879   *Confidence* serialized in *Scribner's* (book published 1880); *Hawthorne* published in English Men of Letters series. Friendships with Edmund Gosse, Robert Louis Stevenson, and the Henry Adamses.

1880–81   Winters in Florence. *Washington Square* serialized in *Cornhill Magazine* and *Harper's* (book published 1880). *The Portrait of a Lady* serialized in *Macmillan's* and the *Atlantic Monthly* (book published 1881).

1881–83   Returns to America; visits family in Boston, meets President Arthur in Washington. Mother dies in early 1882 before he can reach her deathbed. Returns to Europe, until he hears father is dying; arrives in America after father's death in late 1882. Quarrels with William over father's estate, of which he is executor. Brother Garth Wilkinson dies in late 1883. Returns to London. Publishes 14-volume collected edition of works, *The Siege of London;* and *Portraits of Places.*

1884   Visits Paris; renews friendships with French intellectuals. Meets John Singer Sargent; persuades him to take up residence in London. Publishes *Tales of Three Cities,* "The Art of Fiction," and *A Little Tour in France.*

1885   Lives with sister Alice in England. Publishes *The Author of "Beltraffio"* and *Stories Revived. The Bostonians* serialized in *Century* (book published 1886); *The Princess Casamassima* serialized in the *Atlantic Monthly* (book published 1886).

1886–87   Lives in Italy; friendship with James Fenimore Cooper's grand-niece, Constance Fenimore Woolson. Writes "The Aspern Papers," other short stories; begins *The Tragic Muse.*

1888   Publishes *The Reverberator,* "The Aspern Papers," "Louisa Pallant," "The Modern Warning," and *Partial Portraits.*

1889–90   James travels around Europe. Dramatizes *The American*. Friendships with William Morton Fullerton and Wolcott Balestier. *The Tragic Muse* serialized in the *Atlantic Monthly* (book published 1890), which rejects story "The Pupil" (story published in England). Publishes *A London Life*.

1891   Dramatic version of *The American* reasonably popular; James concentrates on drama, which meets with indifferent success. Writes favorably of Ibsen's *Hedda Gabler*.

1892–93   Death of Alice. Travels around Europe; visits with William. Play, *Mrs. Jasper,* produced, but most of the other dramas James writes in these years go unproduced. Publishes *The Lesson of the Master* (1892) and *The Real Thing and Other Tales* (1893).

1894   Constance Fenimore Woolson commits suicide. James receives one of four privately printed copies of Alice's diary; burns it. Publishes *Two Comedies* and *Theatricals*.

1895   Disastrous opening of play *Guy Domville*. Dramatizes some of his fiction. Publishes *Terminations*.

1896–97   *The Spoils of Poynton* serialized in the *Atlantic Monthly* as *The Old Things* (book published 1897). Publishes *Embarrassments*. Friendship with Joseph Conrad. Hires stenographer and buys typewriter. Leases Lamb House in Rye. Publishes *What Maisie Knew*.

1898   "The Turn of the Screw" serialized in *Collier's* (published with "Covering End" as *The Two Magics*). Publishes *In the Cage*. Receives celebrities at Lamb House, including neighbors Stephen Crane and H. G. Wells.

1899   *The Awkward Age* serialized in *Harper's* (book published 1899).

1900   Publishes *The Soft Side*. Lives in Rye and London.

1901   Completes *The Ambassadors*. Publishes *The Sacred Fount*. Obtains permanent room at the Reform Club as London residence.

1902   Publishes *The Wings of the Dove*. Writes "The Beast in the Jungle" and "The Birthplace." Suffers gout and stomach disorders.

1903   Publishes *The Ambassadors, The Better Sort,* and *William Wetmore Story and His Friends*. Friendships with Dudley Jocelyn Persse and Edith Wharton.

1904–5 Publishes *The Golden Bowl* (1904). Returns to America for a visit. Travels around country visiting friends and giving lectures. Elected with William to newly founded American Academy of Arts and Letters; William declines. Returns to England and begins revising his works for the New York edition.

1906–8 Publishes *The American Scene* (1907); writes "The Jolly Corner." The New York edition of James's works is published 1907–9, with eighteen new prefaces by him. Travels around Europe, often with Edith Wharton. Works a little on dramatizations of "Covering End."

1909   Friendship with Bloomsbury Group. Illnesses. Burns correspondence and papers at Rye. Publishes *Italian Hours*.

1910   Ill much of the year; decides it may be form of nervous breakdown. William joins him in traveling to Europe for cure; they learn Robertson has died. James brothers return to America, where William dies. Henry publishes *The Finer Grain* and *The Outcry*.

1911   Receives honorary degree from Harvard. Returns to England, staying in London while working on autobiography.

1913   Publishes *A Small Boy and Others* (autobiography). Friends and admirers subscribe for seventieth-birthday portrait by Sargent; present him with silver-gilt porringer and dish (a "golden bowl"). Visits Lamb House with niece.

1914   Publishes *Notes of a Son and Brother* and *Notes on Novelists*. World War I begins; James does volunteer hospital work, and is elected chairman of the American Volunteer Motor Ambulance Corps in France.

1915–16 Continues war work; becomes English citizen in 1915. Suffers stroke December 1915; awarded Order of Merit on New Year's Day; dies on February 28. His body is cremated and the ashes buried in the family plot in Cambridge, Massachusetts.

Contributors

HAROLD BLOOM, Sterling Professor of the Humanities at Yale University, is the author of *The Anxiety of Influence, Poetry and Repression,* and many other volumes of literary criticism. His forthcoming study, *Freud: Transference and Authority,* attempts a full-scale reading of all of Freud's major writings. A MacArthur Prize Fellow, he is general editor of five series of literary criticism published by Chelsea House. During 1987–88, he served as Charles Eliot Norton Professor of Poetry at Harvard University.

SALLIE SEARS teaches English at the State University of New York at Stony Brook.

PHILIP M. WEINSTEIN teaches at Swarthmore College. His most recent book is *The Semantics of Desire: The Changing Roles of Identity from Dickens to Joyce.*

ALBERT A. DUNN taught English at the University of Virginia. He now teaches at the Fredonia campus of the State University of New York.

RONALD WALLACE is Professor of English at the University of Wisconsin. He is the author of several books on humor in literature, including *The Last Laugh: Form and Affirmation in the Contemporary American Comic Novel.*

MARTIN PRICE is Sterling Professor of English at Yale University. His books include *Swift's Rhetorical Art: A Study in Structure and Meaning, To the Palace of Wisdom: Studies in Order and Energy from Dryden to Blake,* and a number of edited volumes on literature of the seventeenth, eighteenth, and nineteenth centuries.

MICHAEL SEIDEL is Professor of English at Columbia University and

183

the author of *Exile and the Narrative Imagination* and *The Satiric Inheritance, Rabelais to Sterne*.

JULIE RIVKIN, Assistant Professor of English at Connecticut College, received her Ph.D. from Yale University in 1980. Her *PMLA* essay is part of a book in progress, provisionally entitled *False Positions: The Logic of Representation in Henry James's Later Fiction*.

Bibliography

Allen, Elizabeth. *A Woman's Place in the Novels of Henry James*. London: Macmillan, 1984.

Anderson, Charles. *Person, Place, and Thing in Henry James's Novels*. Durham, N.C.: Duke University Press, 1977.

Anderson, Quentin. *The American Henry James*. New Brunswick, N.J.: Rutgers University Press, 1957.

Auchincloss, Louis. *Reading Henry James*. Minneapolis: University of Minnesota Press, 1975.

Beach, Joseph Warren. *The Method of Henry James*. Philadelphia: Saifer, 1954.

———. *The Twentieth-Century Novel: Studies in Technique*. New York: Century, 1932.

Bellringer, Alan W. *The Ambassadors*. London: Allen & Unwin, 1984.

Bennett, Joan. "The Art of Henry James: *The Ambassadors*." *Chicago Review* 9, no. 1 (1956): 12–26.

Berland, Alwyn. *Culture and Conduct in the Novels of Henry James*. Cambridge: Cambridge University Press, 1981.

Bersani, Leo. "The Jamesian Lie." In *A Future for Astyanax*, 128–55. Boston: Little, Brown, 1976.

Blackmur, R. P. *Studies in Henry James*. New York: New Directions, 1983.

Bradbury, Nicola. *Henry James: The Later Novels*. Oxford: Clarendon, 1979.

Brooks, Van Wyck. *The Pilgrimage of Henry James*. New York: Dutton, 1925.

Cargill, Oscar. *The Novels of Henry James*. New York: Macmillan, 1961.

Chase, Richard. "James' *Ambassadors*." In *Twelve Original Essays on Great American Novels*, edited by Charles Shapiro, 124–47. Detroit: Wayne State University Press, 1958.

Chatman, Seymour. *The Later Style of Henry James*. Oxford: Basil Blackwell, 1972.

Crews, Frederick C. *The Tragedy of Manners: Moral Drama in the Later Novels of Henry James*. New Haven: Yale University Press, 1957.

Dupee, F. W. *Henry James*. New York: Dell, 1965.

Durr, Robert A. "The Night Journey in *The Ambassadors*." *Philological Quarterly* 35 (Spring 1972): 137–50.

Edel, Leon. *Henry James: The Master, 1901–1916*. Philadelphia: Lippincott, 1972.

———. Introduction to *The Ambassadors*, by Henry James. Boston: Houghton Mifflin, 1960.

————, ed. *Henry James: A Collection of Critical Essays*. Englewood Cliffs, N. J.: Prentice-Hall, 1963.

Engstrøm, Susanne. "Epistemological and Moral Validity in Henry James's *The Ambassadors.*" *Language and Literature* 1 (1971): 50–65.

Feidelson, Charles. "James and the 'Man of Imagination.' " In *Literary Theory and Structure: Essays in Honor of William K. Wimsatt,* edited by Frank Brady, John Palmer, and Martin Price, 331–52. New Haven: Yale University Press, 1973.

Felman, Shoshana. "Turning the Screw of Interpretation." *Yale French Studies* 55–56 (1977): 94–207.

Fogel, Daniel Mark. *Henry James and the Structure of the Romantic Imagination.* Baton Rouge: Louisiana State University Press, 1981.

Ford, Ford Madox. *Henry James, A Critical Study.* New York: Octagon, 1964.

Gale, Robert E. *The Caught Image: Figurative Language in the Fiction of Henry James.* Chapel Hill: University of North Carolina Press, 1964.

Garis, Robert E. "The Two Lambert Strethers: A New Reading of *The Ambassadors.*" *Modern Fiction Studies* 7 (1961–62): 305–16.

Gindin, James. *Harvest of a Quiet Eye: The Novel of Compassion.* Bloomington: Indiana University Press, 1971.

Goetz, William R. *Henry James and the Darkest Abyss of Romance.* Baton Rouge: Louisiana State University Press, 1986.

Grover, Philip. *Henry James and the French Novel: A Study in Inspiration.* New York: Barnes & Noble, 1973.

Hartstock, Mildred E. "The Dizzying Crest: Strether as Moral Man." *Modern Language Quarterly* 26 (1965): 414–25.

Holland, Laurence. *The Expense of Vision, Essays on the Craft of Henry James.* Princeton: Princeton University Press, 1964.

Hutchinson, Stuart. *Henry James: An American as Modernist.* London: Vision, 1982.

James, Henry. *The Art of the Novel: Critical Prefaces.* Edited by Richard P. Blackmur. New York: Scribner's, 1934.

————. *The Notebooks of Henry James.* Edited by F. O. Matthiessen and Kenneth P. Murdock. New York: Oxford University Press, 1947.

————. *The Novels and Tales of Henry James.* 26 vols. New York: Scribner's, 1907–17.

Jones, Granville H. *Henry James's Psychology of Experience.* The Hague: Mouton, 1975.

Kaston, Carren. *Imagination and Desire in the Novels of Henry James.* New Brunswick, N. J.: Rutgers University Press, 1984.

Knoepflmacher, U. C. " 'O Rare for Strether!': *Antony and Cleopatra* and *The Ambassadors.*" *Nineteenth-Century Fiction* 19 (1965): 333–44.

Krook, Dorothea. *The Ordeal of Consciousness in Henry James.* Cambridge: Cambridge University Press, 1962.

Leavis, F. R. *The Great Tradition: George Eliot, Henry James, Joseph Conrad.* London: Chatto & Windus, 1948.

Lebowitz, Naomi. *The Imagination of Loving: Henry James's Legacy to the Novel.* Detroit: Wayne State University Press, 1965.

Leyburn, Ellen Douglass. *Strange Alloy: The Relation of Comedy to Tragedy in the Fiction of Henry James.* Chapel Hill: University of North Carolina Press, 1968.

Long, R. E. "*The Ambassadors* and the Genteel Tradition: James's Corrections of Hawthorne and Howells." *New England Quarterly* 42 (March 1969): 44–64.

Lubbock, Percy. *The Craft of Fiction*. New York: Scribner's, 1921.

Mackenzie, Manfred. *Communities of Honor and Love in Henry James*. Cambridge: Harvard University Press, 1976.

Marks, Robert. *James's Later Novels*. New York: William-Frederick, 1960.

Matthiessen, F. O. *Henry James: The Major Phase*. New York: Oxford University Press, 1963.

Maugham, W. Somerset. *Ten Novels and Their Authors*. London: Heinemann, 1954.

Norrman, Ralf. *The Insecure World of Henry James's Fiction: Intensity and Ambiguity*. New York: St. Martin's, 1982.

Phelan, James. "Deliberative Acts vs. Grammatical Closure: Stanley Fish and the Language of *The Ambassadors*." In *Worlds from Words: A Theory of Language in Fiction*. Chicago: University of Chicago Press, 1981.

Poirier, Richard. *A World Elsewhere: The Place of Style in American Literature*. New York: Oxford University Press, 1966.

Richards, Bernard. "*The Ambassadors* and *The Sacred Fount*: The Artist Manqué." In *The Air of Reality: New Essays on Henry James*, edited by John Goode, 219–43. London: Methuen, 1972.

Samuels, Charles Thomas. *The Ambiguity of Henry James*. Urbana: University of Illinois Press, 1971.

Schneider, Daniel J. *The Crystal Cage: Adventures of the Imagination in the Fiction of Henry James*. Lawrence, Kans.: Regents Press, 1978.

———. "The Ironic Imagery and Symbolism of James' *The Ambassadors*." *Criticism* 9, (1967): 174–96.

Sharp, Sister M. Corona. *The Confidante in Henry James: Evolution and Moral Value of a Fictive Character*. Notre Dame: University of Indiana Press, 1963.

Shriber, Michael. "Cognitive Apparatus in *Daisy Miller, The Ambassadors* and Two Works by Howells: A Comparative Study of the Epistemology of Henry James." *Language and Style* 2 (1969): 207–25.

Smith, Peter. *Public and Private Value: Studies in the Nineteenth-Century Novel*. Cambridge: Cambridge University Press, 1984.

Spender, Stephen. *The Destructive Element*. London: Jonathan Cape, 1935.

Springer, Mary Doyle. *A Rhetoric of Literary Character: Some Women of Henry James*. Chicago: University of Chicago Press, 1978.

Stallman, R. W. " 'The Sacred Rage': The Time-Theme in *The Ambassadors*." *Modern Fiction Studies* 3 (1957): 41–56.

Stanzel, Franz. *Henry James: The Writer and His Work*. Amherst: University of Massachusetts Press, 1985.

———. *Narrative Situations in the Novel:* Tom Jones, Moby-Dick, The Ambassadors, Ulysses. Bloomington: Indiana University Press, 1971.

Stevenson, Elizabeth. *The Crooked Corridor: A Study of Henry James*. New York: Macmillan, 1949.

Stone, Albert E., ed. *Twentieth Century Interpretations of* The Ambassadors. Englewood Cliffs, N. J.: Prentice-Hall, 1969.

Stone, Edward. *The Battle and the Books: Some Aspects of Henry James*. Athens: Ohio University Press, 1964.

Stowell, Peter H. *Literary Impressionism: James and Chekhov*. Athens: University of Georgia Press, 1980.

Tanner, Tony. "The Watcher from the Balcony: Henry James's *The Ambassadors*." *Critical Quarterly* 8 (1966): 35–52.

Veeder, William. *Henry James: The Lessons of the Master*. Chicago: University of Chicago Press, 1975.

———. "Strether and the Transcendence of Language." *Modern Philology* 69 (1971): 116–32.

Wallace, Ronald. "Comic Form in *The Ambassadors*." *Genre* 5 (1972): 31–50.

Ward, J. A. *The Imagination of Disaster: Evil in the Fiction of Henry James*. Lincoln: University of Nebraska Press, 1961.

———. *The Search for Form: Studies in the Structure of James's Fiction*. Chapel Hill: University of North Carolina Press, 1967.

Watanabe, Hisayoshi. "Past-Perfect Retrospection in the Style of Henry James." *American Literature* 34 (1962–63): 165–81.

Watt, Ian. "The First Paragraph of *The Ambassadors*: An Explication." In *The Ambassadors*, edited by S. P. Rosenbaum. New York: Norton, 1964.

Wegelin, Christof. *The Image of Europe in Henry James*. Dallas: Southern Methodist University Press, 1958.

Winner, Viola Hopkins. *Henry James and the Visual Arts*. Charlottesville: University Press of Virginia, 1970.

Winters, Yvor. "Maule's Well: Or, Henry James and the Relation of Morals to Manners." In *In Defense of Reason*, 300–43. Chicago: Swallow, 1947.

Wolf, H. R. "The Psychology and Aesthetics of Abandonment in *The Ambassadors*." *Literature and Psychology* 21 (1971): 133–47.

Wright, Walter F. *The Madness of Art: A Study of Henry James*. Lincoln: University of Nebraska Press, 1962.

Acknowledgments

"The Negative Imagination: *The Ambassadors*" (originally entitled "*The Ambassadors*)" by Sallie Sears from *The Negative Imagination: Form and Perspective in the Novels of Henry James* by Sallie Sears, © 1968 by Cornell University. Reprinted by permission of the publisher, Cornell University Press.

"Strether's Curious 'Second Wind': Imagination and Experience in *The Ambassadors*" by Philip M. Weinstein from *Henry James and the Requirements of the Imagination* by Philip M. Weinstein, © 1971 by the President and Fellows of Harvard College. Reprinted by permission of Harvard University Press.

"The Articulation of Time in *The Ambassadors*" by Albert A. Dunn from *Criticism* 14, no. 2 (Spring 1972), © 1972 by Wayne State University Press. Reprinted by permission.

"The Major Phase: *The Ambassadors*" by Ronald Wallace from *Henry James and the Comic Form* by Ronald Wallace, © 1975 by the University of Michigan. Reprinted by permission of the University of Michigan Press.

"James: The Logic of Intensity—'Almost Socratic' " by Martin Price from *Forms of Life: Character and Moral Development in the Novel* by Martin Price, © 1983 by Yale University. Reprinted by permission of the author and Yale University Press.

"The Lone Exile: James's *The Ambassadors* and *The American Scene*" by Michael Seidel from *Exile and the Narrative Imagination* by Michael Seidel, © 1986 by Yale University. Reprinted by permission of Yale University Press.

"The Logic of Delegation in *The Ambassadors*" by Julie Rivkin from *PMLA* 101, no. 5 (October 1986), © 1986 by the Modern Language Association of America. Reprinted by permission of the Modern Language Association of America.

Index

Achilles, (*Iliad*), likened to Lambert
 Strether, 134
Aeneid (Virgil), 138
Age of Innocence, The (Wharton), 1
Alcott, Bronson, 2
Amadis of Gaul, 148
Ambassadors, The: character development and purpose in, 8–9, 15–16,
 24–25, 32–34, 50–52, 153–60; as
 comedy of manners, 99–101, 104,
 106, 111, 132, 142, 148; and concept of reward and money, 139–
 43; epic salvation in, 132–33;
 European-American dichotomy in,
 16, 18, 19–21, 22–23, 25, 28, 31,
 42, 69–70, 102, 113, 116, 123–24,
 129–30, 135–36, 141; feudalism in,
 29, 39; irony in, 9, 17, 59, 143–44,
 145–46; logic of supplementarity
 in, 154–69, 163–66; masculine-
 feminine opposition in, 34–37, 42,
 59, 137–39; moral consciousness
 in, 13, 16, 21–23, 51, 83, 103, 113–
 14, 120, 125, 135–36, 151, 167–68;
 motifs of enchantment and imagination vs. experience and action,
 13–14, 30, 33, 48–52, 61, 68, 71–
 73, 76, 79–81, 148–49, 170; Paterian influence in, 9–12; themes of
 youth, age, and renunciation in,
 10–11, 13, 25, 28, 55–57, 63, 70,

75, 77, 79–81, 153–60; time
 schemes in, 83–97, 139–40; tone
 of visionary love, loss, and melan-
 choly in, 10–11, 12, 14–15, 16, 19,
 25, 28, 30–31, 42, 57–58, 63–64,
 70, 97, 175
American, The, 2
American Scene, The, 7–8, 124, 130,
 136, 140
Anderson, Quentin, 78
Antony (*Antony and Cleopatra*), 65
Antony and Cleopatra (Shakespeare), 26,
 65, 130
Archer, Isabel (*The Portrait of a Lady*),
 2, 12, 25, compared to Lambert
 Strether, 8, 32–33, 48–49, 73;
 Emersonian vision of, 7; Protes-
 tant will of, 8; as rebel, 43
Ariel (*The Tempest*), 114
Art of the Novel: Critical Prefaces, The
 (Blackmur), 27, 28, 44
As I Lay Dying (Faulkner), 1
Athena (*Iliad*), 137
Austen Jane, 1, 6; and concept of
 moral life, 5, 18

Barrace, Miss, 62; compared to Lam-
 bert Strether, 69
"Beast in the Jungle, The," 34, 146
Berenson, Bernard, 3